Dear Readers,

I hope you will be inspired by  this cookbook. I have always Eat" and have tried to live my life accordingly. So when parrots joined my family, it was natural to extend the same concepts to their diets as well.

In addition to the physical health benefits, parrots profit mentally from a diet which provides for a variety of choices, textures and tastes. If organic produce is used, parrots can do the work of peeling and manipulating, just as they do in the wild for hours every day. This keeps them mentally occupied in a positive way, which is especially important if they spend many hours without other social activities. Also, if a parrot consumes healthy foods, they will feel better; and when they feel better, they have more potential for positive companionship with us.

I encourage you to make EVERY ingredient in your parrot's diet a healthy one. This means avoiding the abundance of processed foods found in our society, especially foods with processed flours and sugars which consume the inner aisles of our grocery stores.

You may decide that your parrot does not like certain foods. We hear this often, but there is usually a way to motivate every parrot to try new foods and shift to a better diet. Never give up! In this book, thanks to many wonderful contributors, you will find some ideas and foods that may help your parrot to make a shift towards healthier eating.

Remember that food is generated from the resources of our precious planet. I encourage you to support your local farmers to reduce the carbon footprint caused by more extensive transportation; and buy organic when you can to protect the land, and both you and your parrot's health.

I hope you and your birds will enjoy some of these recipes together. Parrots are extremely social, especially at meal time, and will certainly appreciate your efforts to provide healthy, fun foods and share a meal together!

Ann and Phoenix
November 2009

INTRODUCTION

A good diet can help prevent disease and ill health. Food is also restorative, helping our bodies to heal. Providing a parrot with a varied diet is important both for physical nutrition as well as mental joy and satisfaction. Enrich your parrot's life with a plentiful VARIETY of fresh, wholesome foods.

A bird that has a strong preference for only a few food items may likely develop a suppressed immune system, or even be malnourished. Since birds do not usually show illness (this helps them avoid predators in the wild!), you may not be aware of deficiencies until your bird is quite ill. A well-balanced and highly varied diet will not only help prevent illness, but will also support your parrot's immune system which is important during times of stress, molts, surgery etc. Here are some of the important elements of a well-balanced diet.

Make both vitamin A and calcium-rich foods a staple in your bird's daily diet. Calcium-rich foods include carrots, unhulled sesame seeds, broccoli, dandelion and other leafy greens, yogurt and almonds. To absorb calcium, vitamin D3 is needed, which can be acquired directly through ultraviolet light, or as a supplement in some pellets. The best way is to let your parrot enjoy some safe time outdoors or provide access to a full spectrum light.

Foods which help produce vitamin A are also essential for parrots. Deep orange vegetables and fruits are rich in beta carotene (yams, pumpkin, carrots, winter squashes, mango, papaya, apricots and cantaloupe for example) as well as palm oil, leafy greens and broccoli.

Many parrots are grain feeders in the wild, and will enjoy having grain foods upon occasion. These can be cooked, sprouted or simply soaked. There is a wide variety to choose from such as quinoa, groats, spelt, kamut, rice, amaranth, buckwheat and barley. Combine grains along with recommended legumes such as lentil, garbanzo, adzuki or mung for a complete protein. Other sources of protein include cooked salmon or trout, tuna, chicken, chicken bones, quinoa and occasional egg dishes. Most parrots relish these foods and will savor every morsel.

<u>Healthy</u> seeds contribute to the health of your parrot. These include: sprouts,

soaked or sprouted grains, legumes, nuts, pumpkin seeds, flax seeds, and unhulled sesame seeds. Please do not feed your bird only a packaged "bird seed" diet. Not only does this diet lack essential ingredients like vitamin A, calcium and protein, but most packaged seed diets are high in fat and lead to ill health.

Smaller birds such as parakeets, cockatiels and lovebirds need more grains rather than pellets; such as oat groats, flax, canary seed and other grains. Sprouts are especially healthy, action-packed seeds coming to life that are packed with enzymes and great nutrition. You can also simply soak these grains, which brings them to life, and most small birds will find delight in eating these moist morsels.

Fruits are a delectable part of the diet of many parrots. Keep dried fruits to a minimum and make sure they are always unsulfured.

Essential fatty acids (EFAs) support key functions of the body and must be obtained through the diet. High sources of EFAs include flax seeds and oil, walnuts, pumpkin seeds, leafy vegetables and fish.

Parrots evolved to eat natural, unprocessed foods. Look for pellets with organic ingredients (no dyes). Avoid extruded pellets made with heat which greatly lowers the nutritional value.

Change the water frequently to help prevent bacteria, but give your bird a chance to enjoy this "water feature." Many birds take great pleasure in dunking their food or taking a bath in their water dish. If you are gone for extended hours, try a water bottle during your time away, and provide fresh bowls of water at family mealtimes.

Pay attention to what your bird actually eats, not just what you provide. If your parrot has not learned to eat fresh foods, try mixing minced food into pellets or seed, make a warm mash with a favorite item sprinkled on top to create curiosity, or play a game and show your parrot that it is yummy to eat a particular food. Don't give up, your bird can learn to enjoy healthy foods in addition to pellets!

YOU ARE WHAT YOU EAT!

KITCHEN ESSENTIALS

There are several items useful to have on hand for food preparation.

LARGE CAST IRON SKILLET. Cast iron is safe and can be used on the stove-top or in the oven. A large skillet is useful for birdie bread, casseroles or stove-top recipes.

SMALL CAST IRON SKILLET for eggs or small meals made on the stove-top or in the oven.

STAINLESS STEEL 2 QUART SAUCEPAN for cooking grains, legumes and veggies. Better yet, get one that also has a second pan with holes that can be used for steaming. Steaming is not only a great way to cook some veggies, it is also a simple way to quickly warm meals. I prefer this to microwaves, simply because the hot spots created by microwaves can be dangerous for your bird.

SMALL FOOD PROCESSOR for grinding your own flour, making purees from veggies or fruits, finely chopping foods so that picky eaters can't avoid the good stuff, and saving you preparation time for some recipes.

LARGE BOWL for making mashes, or large quantities which can be stored for future use.

SPROUT JAR or SPROUTER Not only are sprouts one of the least expensive and easy foods to make for your parrots, but they are probably the healthiest food you can provide.

NEVER USE NON–STICK COOKWARE WITH PTFE, IT CAN KILL YOUR BIRD!!

SUBSTITUTIONS

The goal is to make sure that every ingredient in your parrot's diet has nutritional value. There are many foods to avoid like chocolate and coffee, but there are also many "foods" that have little-to-no value and can actually be harmful in the long run. These include items like processed sugar or bleached flour, as well as quick-mixes. You can replace oils in baked goods with healthier ingredients. Here are a few ideas for substitutions which can help improve the nutritional value in recipes that call for oil, butter, sugar, milk, processed flours or eggs.

OIL OR BUTTER: For baking, use applesauce in equal portions, or a fruit puree. For cooking in a skillet, coconut oil or palm oil can also be substituted in most cases. Flax oil should never be heated.

EGG: In baking, use 1/3 cup applesauce, or 1/3 cup pumpkin puree, or a small mashed banana.

MILK: Try coconut, oat, almond or rice milk.

SUGAR: Always avoid refined sugar! If you wish to share the recipe with your bird and need more sweetness for yourself, try a puree of fruit, applesauce, or a bit of honey, agave or maple syrup instead.

FLOUR: Refined flour, like refined sugar, is not healthy. For recipes that call for flour, consider making your own by quickly grinding whole oats, quinoa, or even garbanzo beans. In addition, there are some great flours on the market now. Try www.bobsredmill.com for some great ideas.

OTHER HELPFUL TIPS

Feeding twice daily approximates food gathering time periods in the wild. However, parrots spend hours looking for their food, and then using their hookbills to break into a variety of nuts, pods, sprouts, fruits, legumes, grains, bulbs, and tubers. These things take time. What does your bird do all day? For some ideas about how to keep your bird occupied by foraging for food or fun, go to page 13.

Having no food for a couple of hours between meals may allow a bird's body to detoxify itself and build up hunger. It also allows the crop to empty completely, which is also natural.

Be careful not to leave foods that spoil easily in the cage for long periods of time. Cooked foods should be removed after 2 or 3 hours. Raw foods can stay much longer, and are usually safe to provide while you are at work in the daytime, unless you are in a very humid or warm environment. If you are concerned, spritzing raw foods with a small bit of organic apple cider vinegar can help prevent bacterial growth.

Let your bird be "part of the flock" by eating with the family as often as possible. In the wild, birds that live in small groups may still come together in a larger flock while feeding. This gives them a sense of safety from would-be predators. Your parrot is also a very social being, and will truly enjoy this quality time with the family. Many of the recipes in this book are delicious for us as well, so I hope this will encourage you to improve your health at the same time.

Remember that **VARIETY** is important. Every food group, and every food item, has a unique nutritional value. Providing a variety is not only physically important, but it is also mentally enriching. Your bird will enjoy the delicious diversity of taste and textures just as you do! Try not to miss seasonal foods such as cherries, apricots or pomegranates. Your bird will appreciate these special, very healthy annual treats.

ESSENTIAL DIETARY COMPONENTS: CALCIUM

Calcium is a very important component to a bird's diet. There are many calcium-rich foods, which should be available to your bird in abundance. Many of these calcium-rich foods are also high in vitamin A precursors (beta-carotene). Provide some of these every day if possible.

To synthesize calcium, there must be a proper balance between vitamin D3 and calcium levels in the body. Sunlight, or full spectrum light, is the key to this balance. Most pellets have vitamin D supplements, however, access to full spectrum light is highly recommended. Natural sunlight is the best!

Cuttlebone, oyster shells and mineral blocks are not recommended--these are inefficient, unnatural for parrots and their sources are often polluted.

D3 is synthesized in the body by exposure to UV light, and 15-45 minutes a day is reportedly enough for growing chickens. Vitamin D3 precursors may be excreted by the preen gland and spread over the feathers, then reingested.

GOOD SOURCES OF CALCIUM

Almonds	Celery	Kale	Parsnips
Apricots	Collard Greens	Kelp	Romaine Lettuce
Bok Choy	Dandelion	Lemons, Limes	Sesame Seeds
Broccoli	Eggs and Shells	Mustard Greens	Tofu
Cabbage	Figs	Oats	Turnip Greens
Carrots	Hazelnuts	Oranges	Watermelon

ESSENTIAL DIETARY COMPONENTS: OMEGA-3 FATTY ACIDS

- Essential fatty acids (EFAs) are the key building blocks for every cell in the body, and are also important for the assimilation of fat-soluble vitamins. These are the vitamins that cannot be absorbed properly without EFAs.

- Found in flax seed and flax seed oil, dark leafy greens (organic), pumpkin seeds, walnuts, and salmon; as well as hemp, chia, sea buckthorn oils, blueberry, raspberry, kiwi and purslane.

ESSENTIAL DIETARY COMPONENTS:
VITAMIN A

Vitamin A is 'mission essential' for your bird's health. Beta-carotene is a red/orange pigment found in fruits and plants, and it is the precursor to this important vitamin. Once consumed, the liver turns the beta-carotene into vitamin A and stores it for future use. The darker the flesh (the inside, not the skin) of the vegetable or fruit, the higher the beta carotene content. Vegetables can be fed raw but are sometimes more digestible if lightly cooked (steamed or baked by preference). However, note that overcooking can destroy vitamin content.

Green vegetables
- Dandelion greens, collard greens, mustard greens, turnip greens, kale, broccoli, chicory, parsley, green peppers, fennel, romaine, brussel sprouts, beet greens, cabbage, and alfalfa.

Yellow-orange vegetables
- Pumpkin, yams, sweet potatoes, carrots, butternut squash, acorn squash, hot peppers, red peppers.

Fruits with good beta carotene
- Mango, peaches, nectarines, red cherries, apricots, cantaloupe, raw plantain, papaya, pomegranates.

ESSENTIAL DIETARY COMPONENTS:
PROTEIN

Proteins are the building blocks of every cell in our bodies, and the only way to acquire many of the amino acids needed is through diet. Seed-only diets, even if complimented by fruits and vegetables, do NOT provide sufficient protein. Here are some food items which provide protein, and can be fed in moderation.

- Yogurt, low-fat
- Cheese or cottage cheese (great training treats!)
- Well-cooked eggs
- Well-cooked chicken, salmon or white fish (no antibiotics or hormones added, please). Chicken bones are fine. Water-packed tuna.
- Combinations of various grains and legumes (e.g. beans and rice)
- Nuts
- A quality compressed pellet. We do not recommended extruded pellets -- these are made with high heat and the nutritional value is diminished. PLEASE DON'T FEED: Monkey chow, dog food or cat food.

GENERAL INFORMATION
TIPS and IDEAS

- Make Your Own "Casserole" — Page 11
- Why Organic? — Page 12
- Items With The Highest Pesticide Levels — Page 12
- Ways To Disinfect Fruits And Veggies — Page 12
- Teach Your Bird To Try New Things And To Forage — Page 13
- How Does Your Bird Spend the Day? — Page 14
- Multiple Food Stations — Page 16
- Foods Your Bird Should Not Have — Page 16
- Appetizers — Page 17
- Condiments — Page 17
- Essential Fatty Acids (EFAs) — Page 18
- Ginger, Milk Thistle, Kelp — Page 18
- Cinnamon, Cayenne, Garlic — Page 19
- Sesame Seed, Celery Seed, Cilantro / Coriander — Page 20
- Coriander Chelation Pesto — Page 20
- Alfalfa, Dandelion, Aloe Vera — Page 21
- Probiotics — Page 22
- Do You Have A Feather Plucker? — Page 22
- What Is A Seed? — Page 23
- Soaking — Page 23
- Sprouting — Page 23-25
- Palm Oil, Coconut Oil, Juice — Page 26
- Flowers And Plants, Pinecones — Page 27
- Plants And Parrots – A Personal Perspective — Page 28-31
- Container Gardens For Parrots — Page 32-33

MAKE YOUR OWN "CASSEROLE"

When you are away at work or for several hours, only leave fresh uncooked foods. One approach is to provide pellets and an assortment of fruits and vegetables in the morning. The evening is a perfect time to share a cooked meal. Be creative by combining ingredients from different food groups. Many of the recipes in this book can be cooked in advance and stored in the refrigerator or freezer for future use. Top with a favorite condiment when serving and enjoy! You can create your own dishes by choosing from the food groups below.

Larger birds may appreciate chunks they can pick up and manipulate, smaller birds may prefer everything chopped up in small pieces. For picky birds, blend the items together into a "mash" so they can are sure to eat the good things too.

VEGETABLES GREEN: Dandelion greens, purslane, collard greens, mustard greens, turnip greens, kale, chard, romaine, broccoli, chicory, parsley, green peppers, fennel, brussel sprouts, beet greens, snap peas, green beans, cabbage and alfalfa. YELLOW-ORANGE-RED: Yams, sweet potatoes, carrots, butternut squash, pumpkin, acorn squash, hot peppers, red and yellow peppers, beets and radish. OTHER: Turnip, daikon, cucumber and okra.

FRUIT Mango, apricots, cantaloupe, kiwi, papaya, pomegranates, blueberries, raspberries, cranberries, pineapple, bananas, peaches, nectarines, cherries, oranges and plums. <u>Dried fruits should always be unsulfured!</u>

LEGUMES
- Sprouted mung, adzuki, lentil, green pea or garbanzo beans.
- Cooked mung, adzuki, lentil, green pea or garbanzo beans.
- Other beans such as black, cannelini, pinto, kidney or navy must be very well cooked to be non-toxic. Not recommended on a regular basis.

GRAINS Quinoa, groats, spelt, kamut, brown rice, amaranth, buckwheat, unhulled barley, millet, oat, French couscous, Israeli couscous, gluten-free pasta and canary seed. (TIP: Birds love pasta, but this carbohydrate should be minimized, especially pasta made with bleached flours).

PROTEIN Fish, chicken, eggs, organic compressed pellets without dyes, nuts (walnut, brazil, hazelnut, almond, pecan), pumpkin seeds, yogurt, cheese (limited), beans and legumes combos, quinoa and limited sunflower seed (best sprouted).

General Information, Tips and Ideas, 11

WHY ORGANIC?

Of all the food groups, PRODUCE has the highest incidence of pesticide and chemical residue. Pesticides have been linked with cancer, neurological problems, hormonal imbalances and immune system problems. Growth hormones and antibiotics are found in most non-organic meats and dairy products.

Organic foods contain many more nutrients and taste better! The skin can be left on most organic fruits and vegetables, and this provides birds an opportunity to manipulate their own food, an activity both physically and mentally enriching. The peel also contains some of the highest levels of nutrients.

WHICH ITEMS HAVE THE HIGHEST PESTICIDE LEVELS?

To obtain a current list of the produce with the highest pesticide levels as listed by the Environmental Working Group, go to: www.foodnews.org/

The most recent "dirty dozen" as of March 10, 2009 are: peach, apple, bell pepper, celery, nectarine, strawberries, cherries, kale, lettuce, grapes (imported), carrot and pear.

If you were asked to list a dozen of the NON-ORGANIC fruits and vegetables that you offer your parrots most often, how many of these would be included? We recommend you buy organic produce as often as possible, and especially those on the top dozen with the highest pesticide levels.

Many scientists now acknowledge that even small amounts of pesticides can cause serious harm. These studies assume that the produce was rinsed and peeled, so this does not eliminate the pesticide levels.

WAYS TO DISINFECT FRUITS AND VEGGIES

1. OXYFRESH Cleansing Gele. Just use a drop per large bowl and soak the produce for a few minutes. Rinse well. A bottle of Oxyfresh goes a long way. It can also be used to clean cages and for many other household cleaning chores.

2. GSE-Grapefruit Seed Extract. Only a few drops needed. RINSE WELL. GSE also inhibits the growth of mold and fungus. GSE can kill many bacteria, including strep. However, it also kills good bacteria, so make sure to rinse well before ingesting.

3. VINEGAR (organic raw apple cider). 1 part vinegar to 3 parts water. Spray or put in large bowl and let sit for 5 minutes. Rinse.

TEACH YOUR BIRD
TO TRY NEW THINGS and TO FORAGE

- Go organic when possible so you can give your parrot a job by leaving skins on, or providing bigger chunks of food that they must manipulate.
- Mix the healthy things (like chopped greens) with the more favorite food items.
- Provide food diversity and put the food items in different places, heights and bowls.
- Use corn husks or small pieces of tortilla to wrap up healthy food items
- Fill a red or green pepper with chopped fresh foods and hang from a skewer.
- Skewer whole food items like: orange, pear, squash, pumpkins, greens wrapped around nuts, green or red pepper filled with other goodies. Weave leafy greens (organic dandelion, kale, collard, etc) in and out of the cage bars.
- Hang a whole item from the top like a carrot, or an upside down beet with leafy greens, or a big dripping wet collard greens.
- Put rocks or wooden balls on top of the food in the bowl.
- Put a tablespoon of quality seed on the food. Your bird will root around and eat other good things in the process.
- Show your parrot that a type of food is "safe" and good. Take a bite and make BIG DRAMATIC YYUUUMMM sounds.
- Give a piece to another parrot who likes this food. Teach through modeling and vicarious learning.
- Put various foods in different places in the cage. Make foraging fun.
- Put the new food in a food the parrot already likes (e.g. birdie bread, omelet, soup, juice, etc).
- Make a layered salad and chop it up so it is mixed with other favored ingredients.
- Teach by positive reinforcement. Incrementally: show your bird the food - Praise. Touch the food to your parrot's beak - Praise. When your bird touches the food with her tongue - Praise. Be patient, immediate and consistent with the praise and each step of learning.
- Hide food in a paper bag. Put some yogurt or almond butter on a hanging stainless steel spoon. Stuff some fresh carrots or greens

General Information, Tips and Ideas, 13

into a recycled plastic container.
- Put some safe, fresh branches in the cage and hang foods from these.
- Use a foraging cage and fill it with assorted fresh foods.

For more great enrichment ideas, Kris Porter has developed some exceptional materials. Go to:

ParrotEnrichment.com or phoenixlanding.org/PEAB_V2.pdf
A VERY special thanks to Kris for all her support and help with this book!

HOW DOES YOUR BIRD SPEND THE DAY?

A flock of wild Pionus parrots was observed in Ecuador. This was their daily routine:

Dawn to 10:00 A.M.	Foraging for food
10:00 A.M. to 2:00 P.M.	Resting, napping, preening, socializing
2:00 P.M. to 6:00 P.M.	Foraging for food
6:00 P.M. to 6:00 A.M.	Roosting, sleeping

In the wild, parrots:
- Search for the food (TRAVEL)
- Make selection decisions (CHOOSE)
- Show many food manipulation behaviors (MANIPULATE)

In captivity, parrots need to:
- Search for food (be provided mental and physical ACTIVITIES)
- Make selection decisions (have many CHOICES)
- Pick-up, peel, or break open her food (MANIPULATE)

"Most parrot guardians offer food in a dish within the bird's cage, cutting this "foraging time" down to less than 10% of a bird's day vs. the natural 70%. So what's left for the parrot to do? Preen its feathers, sleep, and vocalize…. What does that lack of time doing natural behaviors cause?"

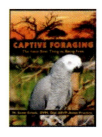

SCOTT ECHOLS, DVM

14, General Information, Tips and Ideas

It is estimated that parrots spend 50-70% of their day in the wild foraging for food. This involves searching for available sources, choosing the most desirable items, and then manipulating the chosen food with their feet and beaks.

Go organic and give your parrot a job. When produce is free of pesticides and fertilizers, then your parrot can do the peeling. Food that is free of growth hormones or antibiotics is also safer for your parrot's long-term health. Teach your parrot to try new foods in addition to daily staples. Make mealtimes a flock-family occasion and enjoy fun times together. Just being together without over-petting is one of the best ways to enjoy companionship with each other.

Parrots need stimulating interaction from their environment. To keep them interested, try teaching birds to:
* Spread their wings, jump, whistle or wave on cue.
* Eat with a spoon, drink from a cup, or other fun behaviors that also help come medicine time.
* Flap, turn somersaults, dance or jump for much needed, good exercise.

To encourage parrots to interact and have fun, try:
* Singing to them, especially songs with their names; imitate each other, copy what your bird says.
* Playing peek-a-boo behind a towel to make the towel less threatening to your bird; or playing "where's parrot?" with a small mirror.
* Whispering things like "parrot" which helps reduce screaming too.
* Playing a catch game. Many birds will throw objects back to you with little training.
* Playing real estate: take your bird around the house and show her each room. This helps decrease anxiety by exploring the surrounding "territory."
* Spending mealtimes together. For birds in the wild, this is their most social time.
* Training husbandry behaviors like going into a carrier, filing nails or going onto a scale.

General Information, Tips and Ideas, 15

MULTIPLE FOOD STATIONS

A simple way to provide foraging opportunities is to use multiple bowls, randomly placed throughout the cage. Start with easy to reach places, and then gradually make it more challenging. Not only does this provide an opportunity for exercise, but your birds will stay busy in a positive way when they are "working" for their food.

Multiple food stations: Include several bowls of food in the cage at various levels and places. In each dish, put a different variety of foods (e.g. peas and cherries in one, squash and banana in another, etc). This will stimulate your parrot to begin looking around and exploring. Spread out the favorite foods amongst the different bowls or foraging toys. Once a parrot is used to the multiple feeding locations, you can make it more challenging by placing the bowls in places that are harder to reach, or put a piece of paper on top to "hide" the food from view.

When you first begin hiding things or making it harder to see into a bowl easily, be patient and give your parrot a few days to become used to the idea of not "seeing" the food. Use beads or polished rocks to cover the food. Your parrot now knows that there "could" be food in that bowl but this provides more of a foraging challenge. Parrots work for their food in the wild, this takes energy and provides mental activity. Both are good for the birds in our homes!

FOODS YOUR BIRD SHOULD NOT HAVE:

- Alcohol of ANY kind (deadly);
- Carbonated soft drinks (too much sugar, acid)
- Avocado, raw onion, rhubarb
- Chocolate
- Caffeine, in any form
- Processed meats (high in fat, salt and additives) or ANY food containing nitrates, sulfites or MSG.
- Chemical dyes (some pellets)
- Processed sugars and flours. Avoid commercial mixes with additives.
- Peanuts not recommended--may be contaminated with aspergillus and they produce a carcinogen called aflotoxin.
- Cow's milk (avian digestive systems do not digest lactose, as differentiated from lactase in yogurt)
- Other processed foods, especially fast foods, high carb foods and ANY with high fructose corn syrup.

APPETIZERS

Does your parrot get a bit more vocal at dinner time, or dusk? This is a natural behavior. In order to reduce dysfunctional screaming, give your parrot a round of "appetizers" while you're preparing dinner. This is also a good way to show them that certain foods are fun and safe. Good appetizers include a piece of broccoli or other raw veggie, a chunk of fruit, a whole nut, banana chips, a piece of rice cake with almond butter and applesauce, etc. Make these healthy appetizers so you won't "spoil" their dinner!

CONDIMENTS

Condiments are a great way to add supplements or variety to your parrot's diet. Also, certain condiments can serve as a great incentive, by encouraging your bird to dive in to a meal and taste new things. When a bird is hesitant to eat healthy foods or something new, we can make it more appealing. Experiment with some of these choices and see how your bird responds.

- Cereals like granola or flakes. Make sure these are not fortified and do NOT contain sugar or fructose corn syrup. Find a brand, preferably organic, with simple natural ingredients.
- Pumpkin Seeds (pepitos). High in Omega-3
- Unhulled Sesame Seeds. High in calcium
- Sprinkled cinnamon or a cinnamon stick
- Chopped GREENS! High in calcium and Vitamin A
- Coconut sprinkles or chunks
- Sprinkled kelp
- Dulse, sea buckthorn
- Flax seeds or flax oil
- Soaked seeds or sprouts. Potent enzymes!
- Unpeeled garlic clove, or minced garlic
- Dry Seeds (millet, safflower, sunflower, groats...)
- Yogurt
- Probiotics
- Cilantro, parsley, basil, celery seed, cayenne, turmeric
- Sprinkle of alfalfa
- Small pieces of fish or chicken
- A chicken bone
- Cheese
- Rolled oats
- Nuts
- Favorite pellets

General Information, Tips and Ideas, 17

⚠ ESSENTIAL FATTY ACIDS (EFAs)

EFAs are unsaturated fats which support the key functions of the body - Omega-3, 6 and 9. Omega-3 is the most important missing ingredient in many of our diets. It used to be readily accessible from organic greens, but we eat less greens than we should, and often from farms where the soil has been depleted of nutrients.

The body does not make EFAs, these must be obtained from the diet.

Best sources for Omega-3 fatty acids are: fresh whole foods, especially: walnuts and Brazil nuts, pumpkin seeds, dark green leafy vegetables (especially dandelions), salmon, tuna, trout, flax seeds, kelp, legumes and oats.

We need EFAs to absorb vitamin A (a fat-soluble vitamin), and vitamin A is especially important for parrots.

Ideal ratio would be 4:1 Omega-3 to Omega 6. Recommended amount if using an oil: 2 drops per day per 500 grams of weight

EFAs cannot be used for cooking. DO NOT HEAT!

GINGER
- Anti-inflammatory, may help with arthritis
- Helps reduce nausea for parrots with motion sickness.

TEA FOR TRAVELING:
Steep 2-3 slices of fresh ginger root in hot water for fifteen minutes. Or add fresh ginger to the food and drinking water several hours before the trip. Some parrots will even munch on it to quell their queasiness.

MILK THISTLE
- Many parrots have liver problems based on poor diet
- Milk thistle protects and shields the liver
- Even rebuilds the cells and restores liver function
- VERY helpful after a course of antibiotics, which are hard on the liver
- Use as a CONDIMENT on fresh foods.
- Parrots will enjoy having "seed"!

KELP

Kelp is a great source of iodine. It comes in powder or granules and can be found in some bulk sections. You can add a sprinkle every day.

CINNAMON

The inner bark of a tropical evergreen tree, harvested during the rainy season when pliable and then dried into curls and sold as sticks or ground into a powder.

Cinnamon has several benefits:
- Lowers cholesterol
- Helps yeast infections
- Has anti-inflammatory qualities that can lessen joint and muscle pain, especially the joint pain associated with arthritis.
- Inhibits bacteria growth and spoilage
- Great source of manganese, fiber, iron, and calcium

CAYENNE

- Also known as capsicum, cayenne is an overall digestive aid

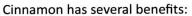

- Contains liberal amounts of vitamins A, C, B-complex, calcium, phosphorous and iron
- Also an anti-inflammatory and helps arthritic conditions
- Some parrots love the fiery taste of cayenne and may try new and unfamiliar foods, such as sprouts, when you sprinkle on this healthful pepper
- Rich in calcium and vitamins A and C, and calcium. Great for the heart, liver, arthritis, and high cholesterol

GARLIC

- Garlic has been shown to contain 18 anti-viral, anti-fungal and anti-bacterial substances
- Stimulates the immune system and kills parasites
- Helps protect the liver and eliminate toxins from body tissues
- A natural antibiotic which is safe for our parrots
- High in calcium
- Lowers cholesterol
- Has anti-atherosclerotic properties
- Neutralizes aspergillus fungus

GIVE YOUR BIRDS GARLIC CLOVES AND LET THEM DO THE PEELING!

General Information, Tips and Ideas,

SESAME SEED, UNHULLED

- One of the oldest condiments
- Very high in calcium and trace minerals
- Unhulled has much higher calcium content (88 mg of calcium per tablespoon for unhulled versus 37 mg for hulled)

CELERY SEED

- Excellent for arthritis
- Also reduces gout/uric acid
- Lowers blood pressure
- Reduces cholesterol

CILANTRO

- Cilantro also helpful in clearing up viral or bacterial infections
- Removes heavy metals from the nervous system and body tissue

CORIANDER CHELATION PESTO

- 4 cloves garlic
- ⅓ cup Brazil nuts (selenium)
- ⅓ cup sunflower seeds (cysteine)
- ⅓ cup pumpkin seeds (zinc, magnesium)
- 2 cups packed fresh coriander leaves (cilantro, Chinese parsley) (vitamin A)
- ⅔ cup flaxseed oil
- 4 tablespoons lemon juice (vitamin C)
- 2 teaspoon dulse powder

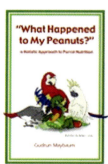

Process the coriander and flaxseed oil in a blender until the coriander is chopped. Add the garlic, nuts and seeds, dulse and lemon juice and mix until the mixture is finely blended into a paste. Store in a dark glass jar if possible. It freezes well, so purchase coriander in season and fill enough jars to last through the year.

Recipe developed by Gudrun Maybaum, Totally Organics (www.totallyorganics.com). Reprinted with permission. Gudrun's nutrition book called "What Happened to my Peanuts?" is also a great resource!

ALFALFA

- Leaves are rich in minerals and nutrients including calcium, magnesium, potassium, and carotene, as well as vitamins A, K and D
- Alkalizes and detoxifies the body, especially the liver
- Contains an anti-fungal agent
- Appetite stimulant, alfalfa is an excellent source of chlorophyll
- Alfalfa seeds contain a slightly toxic amino acid unless used in sprouted form

One option is to keep chopped organic alfalfa leaves in a shaker and use it once or twice a week.

DANDELION

Member of the sunflower family. Birds enjoy the flowers and the leaves.

- Very nutritious! Nature's richest vegetable source of beta carotene (more than carrots)
- HIGH in calcium
- Full of vitamins A, B1, C, D, calcium and potassium
- Helps prevent arthritis
- Helps reduce gout and uric acid
- Excellent for liver disorders

DO NOT PICK DANDELIONS FROM YOUR YARD IF IT HAS BEEN SPRAYED WITH PESTICIDES IN RECENT YEARS!!

ALOE VERA

Aloe stimulates the immune system.

- Add to drinking water occasionally (one part aloe juice to three parts pure water). Find organic aloe with the highest concentration of aloe, and the least additives
- Aloe is a natural anti-histamine, may help prevent feather destruction by inhibiting the release of histamines responsible for skin irritation and itching
- Another form of aloe treatment for feather plucking is aloe spray. It helps to alleviate itching and irritated skin
- Parrots can eat thin slices of fresh aloe as a preventive or curative remedy
- May prevent infection in skin wounds. It draws infection out of wounds as it regenerates healthy tissue

General Information, Tips and Ideas, 21

PROBIOTICS

Beneficial bacteria crowd out disease-causing organisms and make the digestive system less favorable for harmful bacteria and yeast.

Lactobacillus acidophilus replaces the "friendly" intestinal bacteria destroyed by antibiotics. We are still learning about bird flora (versus mammals), and avian medicine is steadily making incredible new improvements.

Times that a probiotic might be useful:

- After any antibiotic treatment to restore healthy bacteria
- Stressed or sick birds
- Before, during, and after a molt
- Helps with plugged or vents pasted with droppings
- Aging birds

DO YOU HAVE A FEATHER PLUCKER?

There are many possible causes of feather destructive behavior, and we still have much to learn. One possible cause could be a food allergies. Here are some foods that MAY coincide with feather plucking, although scientific data is still sparse. Try eliminating these foods from your bird's diet to test for possible improvement. At the same time, try to offer a wholesome diet comprised of fresh fruits, vegetables, grains, legumes and don't forget the Omega-3s and protein - important ingredients for growing feathers! Flax seeds and oil, walnuts, organic leafy greens and pumpkin seeds are high in Omega 3s. Eggs, quinoa and other grain/legume combos provide quality protein.

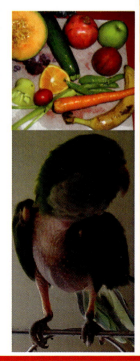

- Preservatives, chemicals, processed foods, dyes
- Wheat (does not include buckwheat grains)
- Corn
- Soy
- Peanuts
- Spirulina
- Refined sugar and flour
- Grease (e.g. french fries)
- Dairy, other than yogurt
- Extruded pellets
- Semolina (in wheat-based pasta)
- Sunflower seeds
- Carbohydrates in general

WHAT IS A SEED?

In most plants, the "seed" gives rise to a new individual, it is the beginning of life. In flowering plants, the seed is enclosed within the fruit. A seed can be any part of a plant such as a bulb, tuber or spore that is used for propagation.

Examples of seeds include: nuts, pods, sprouts, fruits, legumes, grains, bulbs and tubers. These are all nutritious foods for your parrots. This does not include bird seed bought in the pet section at grocery stores!

Parrots are believed to have evolved hookbills in order to break into seeds. These fibrous foods are thought to comprise a large portion of a parrot's diet in the wild.

SOAKING

Many grains can be soaked, which in essence brings them to "life." For a meal, soak a small amount, as needed for one or two feedings, for 10-15 hours. The little birds especially enjoy soaked grains. Try these for the best results: oat groats, kamut, brown rice, millet, unhulled barley, rye, spelt or buckwheat.

SPROUTING

One very nutritious way for a parrot to eat "seeds" is by sprouting. Not only are sprouts super rich in live enzymes, as living plants, but sprouts can be one of the least expensive, organic foods available. Grains and legumes can be bought in bulk or on-line.

One teaspoon of dried grains or legumes will make several teaspoons of sprouts. They are easy to grow, and best of all, uncontaminated by pesticides and other chemicals when we grow them ourselves. In addition, many birds will eat sprouts readily with no hesitation.

We recommend you grow your own sprouts. This is a living food with a short shelf life, and spoil quickly if not attended to properly. Sprouts sold in the grocery store had transport time and may have been on the shelf for a while.

> "Dried seeds are like little treasure chests, containing all the nutrients for a plant to live & grow. Through soaking, we awaken these dormant treasures. After about 12-15 hours of soaking, most seeds are loaded with vitamins, minerals, enzymes, chlorophyll, amino acids, fatty acids and more – in a form that is easy to utilize for the body." Gudrun Maybaum, *What Happened to My Peanuts?*

General Information, Tips and Ideas, 23

SPROUTING
WHAT and HOW
by Laura Ford

Grasses & Grains
- Amaranth: soak 3-5 hours, harvest 2-3 days.
- Barley, hulless type: vitamins A, B complex, E, calcium, iron, magnesium and phosphorus. Glucans to help lower cholesterol and build the immune system. Soak 6 hours, harvest 2-3 days.
- Buckwheat, hulled: soak 6 hours, harvest 3-4 days.
- Millet, unhulled: vitamin B, E, protein. Soak 8 hours, ready in 2-3 days.
- Oats, hulled: vitamin E. Good for immune system and skin disorders unless bird is sensitive to gluten. Soak 8 hours, ready in 1-2 days.
- Quinoa: vitamins B1, B2, B3, B6, folacin, copper, iron, magnesium, phosphorus, potassium, zinc and protein. Soak 3-4 hours, harvest 1-2 days.
- Teff: soak 3-4 hours, harvest 1-2 days.
- Wheat: B complex, E, folacin, iron, magnesium, manganese, protein and Omega-6. Flavor is sweetest when tail first appears. Soak for 12 hours, harvest in 2-3 days.

Legumes. Must be fully sprouted!
- Adzuki bean: vitamin C, iron and protein. Soak 5 hours, harvest 3-5 days.
- Alfalfa sprouts are not only a good source of vitamin C and B, but also beta carotene (vitamin A). If you decide to sprout alfalfa be sure not to feed dormant seeds as the dormant seed contains canavanine, a natural toxin and carcinogen; but when the seed sprouts, any amount is miniscule. Soak 4-6 hours and they should be ready in 4-6 days.
- Fenugreek: iron, phosphorus and trace elements. Soak 6 hours, ready in 2-5 days.
- Lentil sprouts: the richest sprout source of high quality protein (but incomplete, needs to be combined with a grain), approximately 24% protein. Folic acid, C, E, iron, phosphorus and potassium. Soak for 4-12 hours. Harvest in 3-5 days.
- Mung bean sprouts: vitamin A, C, phosphorus and iron. Soak 12 hours; sprouts quickly, but 5 days to get long tails. It may be best to avoid mung beans if a bird has candida or any other yeast type of infection.
- Peas: vitamin A, iron, potassium, magnesium and beta carotene. Contains all 8 essential amino acids and 22% protein. Soak time: 8 hours, harvest in 2-3 days.

Seeds & Nuts
- Almond: B complex, E, calcium, magnesium, potassium, selenium, protein and fatty acids. Soak 8-10 hours, ready to eat.
- Pumpkin seed: B complex, E, phosphorus, iron, zinc, protein. Soak 8 hours, ready in 1 day.
- Sunflower: B complex, D, E, calcium, iron, phosphorus, potassium, magnesium, unsaturated fatty acids and protein. Soak 6-8 hours, harvest in 1-2 days.
- Sesame: B complex. Soak 2-8 hours, ready in 1-2 days.

Herbs & Spices
- Mustard seeds sprouts can add some zesty flavor but when seeds come into contact with water allyl isothiocyanate is formed. Mustard seed sprouts are likely safe but some people prefer to avoid them for their birds. Soak 4-6 hours and harvest in 4-5 days.

Vegetables
- Broccoli seeds: Soak in warm water 8 hours, ready in 1-2 days.
- Radish seeds: vitamins A, C (more than 29 times the vitamin C and 4 times the vitamin A of milk), calcium and protein. Soak 6 hours, harvest 3-5 days.
- Cabbage seeds: Beta Carotene. Soak 8-12 hours and ready in 4 – 6 days.

Seeds to avoid
- Sorghum, aka "super millet" contains cyanide that becomes activated by sprouting to a toxic fatal level.
- Large Beans such as anasazi, black, fava, kidney, navy, pinto, and soy, remain toxic even after full sprouting. If fed (which is not recommended), must be soaked for a minimum of 8 hours, rinsed and cooked well for at least 30 minutes.

How to Sprout
These directions are based on using a quart-sized mason jar with straining lid, or cheese cloth tied around the top of the jar, but the same principles apply to the sprouting cup.

1) Measure 1/2 to 1/3 cup of desired sprout seeds into the container.
2) Rinse the seeds.
3) Fill the container with cool water.
4) Allow to soak for 8 to 12 hours.
5) Rinse and drain. Repeat. Repeat.
6) Lay the jar on its side, away from direct sunlight.
7) Repeat the rinse and drain step 2 to 3 times a day.
8) Sprouts are usually ready to eat in 2 to 3 days (varies by grain or legume)
9) Unused sprouts can be refrigerated at this point.

Note: If at any time the sprouts smell sour or unpleasant, throw them out and start over.

General Information, Tips and Ideas, 25

PALM OIL

Red palm oil is a rich source of vitamin A in the form of carotenoids. These are the yellow to red pigments nutritionally important to many animals; for example, this is what gives flamingos their color. Palm oil is also a wonderful natural source of Vitamin E.

COCONUT OIL

Coconut oil has components (48% lauric acid) to fight viruses and protozoa and parasites such as giardia.

It also has components (7% caprylic acid) to fight yeast (Candida).

Coconut is a powerful tool against immune diseases, and can contribute to building the immune system.

Lastly, it can assist in killing Candida (yeast) and bad bacteria in the digestive tract without hurting the good bacteria.

JUICE

Parrot bodies are built to absorb their vitamins, minerals and enzymes from live plants.

Having trouble getting your parrot to eat their fruits and veggies? Juice might be a fun way to teach your bird to enjoy the taste of healthy produce. It is also a vitamin/mineral/enzyme cocktail for your parrot.

Dr. David McCluggage, a highly respected holistic veterinarian of Colorado, says that apples are always a good first choice for juicing. He also recommends carrots, kale and other healthful fruits and vegetables. Offer the remaining pulp or fibrous leftovers in a separate dish or baked into birdie bread. For more information, see Dr. McCluggage's book, *Holistic Care for Parrots.*

If using bottled or packaged juice, make sure it is pure with NO additives, especially sugars or fructose corn syrup!

Juice can be used as a substitute for water in some recipes, or mix part juice and part water. Carrot juice or mango juice are particularly good for cooking grains.

FLOWERS AND PLANTS

Many parrots enjoy eating bark, flowers and dirt (geophagy) in the wild. We certainly cannot replicate wild diets for parrots in captivity, we can provide them with opportunities to enjoy some flowers and plants in addition to vegetables and fruits.

Edible flowers are often available at grocery stores, but make sure that they are organically grown, and never feed flowers purchased from a florist!

Common flowers enjoyed by parrots are: Aloe Vera Flower, Basil, Bee Balm, Blackberry, Borage, Butterfly Bush, Calendula, Chamomile, Chrysanthemum, Dandelion, Daylily, Dianthus (Carnations, Pinks, Sweet William), Fennel, Dill Flower, Echinacea, Evening Primrose, Garlic, Hibiscus, Lavender, Lilac, Marigolds, Nasturtium, Pansy, Peppermint, Pomegranate, Red Clover, Rose Of Sharon (Hardy Hibiscus), Rose, Rosemary, Sage, Squash Blossoms, Sunflower, Violet, Yarrow and Yerba Santa.

In addition, many trees provide safe perch material, and most birds enjoy chewing bark, shredding it and having different sizes to exercise their feet. Give your parrot an array of branches from safe woods. One of the best perches for your bird's feet is a natural wood perch. Because it is not uniform, it gives the feet a change in shape and improves dexterity.

PINECONES

Find pinecones in good condition. Place in oven heated at 200 degrees for 20 minutes. Turn off the oven and leave the pinecones inside for at least 2 hours to dry out. Do not heat at higher than 200 degrees!

You can also soak pinecones in a bowl of warm water with 1/2 cup vinegar, or run them through the dishwasher if there is no soap or rinse agent. Cones will close up when wet, but they will dry in a few hours.

PLANTS AND PARROTS – A PERSONAL PERSPECTIVE, by Ruth Fahrmeier

I am not a toxicologist or a professional horticulturist; just a long time gardener who has fallen in love with parrots. Over the last few years I have gathered information about plants and parrots. My search for ways to incorporate plants and gardening into the lives of my parrots is not finished, but I have reached a place where I feel that I have enough information to form some opinions and be comfortable allowing my parrots to play and chew on a number of plants. I would like to share the results of my search.

At the end are some web sites with extensive listings of toxic and safe plants and other related material. (With sincere thanks to all of the authors who contributed to my education!) These, just a few of the sites that are out there, I have found particularly helpful and reliable. Even so, you will see some differences among the lists. It is best to avoid any plant that is on the toxic side of any list, until you learn the reason why the plant is sometimes considered toxic and sometimes safe. Then, you can decide if your intended use of that plant will be safe for your feathered friends. Note: A last minute "Google" search turned up a site that includes four plants I have considered safe on the "unsafe" list. They are indicated with an asterisk(*). For myself, I will continue to use these plants because of my personal experience and the fact that the lists I have learned to rely on consider them to be safe. But, please, after you have read the materials, make your own decisions based on your individual parrots and how comfortable you are with the issues involved.

This is a thumbnail sketch of some basic principles I have found and I hope it will be a helpful beginning for you. Basic Principles are: The plant itself must not be toxic to parrots. The plant should be free of pesticides, especially systemic ones. Soil should not have chemical additives, such as slow release fertilizer, or must be completely inaccessible to the parrot. Containers should be made of material that is not toxic to parrots or be out of reach. Location and placement of a plant is important for your parrot's safety and the survival of the plant, unless you consider the plant disposable. Safe plants include some common and easily grown plants such as: spider plant, jade, corn plant*, dracaena*, pony tail palm, impatiens*, Swedish ivy, snap

 dragon, hibiscus*, and nasturtium. Some vegetables (kales, edible flowering cabbage) are attractive and nutritious. Some plants are part safe and part dangerous. The leaves and stems of plants that produce safe and healthy fruits, such as the tomato and its relatives, mango, peaches, plums and cherries are toxic. Some plants that are not toxic can cause physical injury. Young citrus plants and bougainvilleas have sharp thorns. The thorns can be removed. Accurate identification of a plant is important. Many plants have a variety of common names. So, check for the scientific name. You can "Google" to find plant identification sites or catalogues that show pictures.

Branches from woody plants, shrubs and trees make fun perches and stands. Lilac, butterfly bush, dogwood, birch, pine, poplar, and willows are excellent sources. Outside plants need special preparation to make sure bugs, bird droppings and other contaminants that may harm parrots have been removed. There are a number of approaches. (See references page 31.) Grapefruit seed extract (GSE), Oxyfresh Gele, and vinegar are recommended cleaning agents. Scrub, rinse, and dry. A note on pine: the sticky sap can mess up feathers, so peel the bark and let the branches age until they are no longer sticky.

Pesticides can make a safe plant dangerous. You can grow plants from seed or take your own cuttings. When you buy plants, ask the nursery about the use of pesticides. Once you have healthy plants established, a good spray with water keeps many pests off. (Parrots can enjoy a shower at the same time, weather permitting.) In the summer when my plants go outside or on the porch, the good bug population (ladybugs and the like) take over the job. At your discretion, you may decide you need to use some of the natural insecticides based on garlic, hot peppers and the like. Make sure your parrot does not breathe the vapors if you spray your plants.

The soil in which plants grow can pose a danger. My personal choice is to use soil made of natural materials without chemical fertilizers. Identifying such soils and sources is not always easy. Ask and read labels carefully. Be aware that soils might be safe for mammals, but may contain materials that are not safe for parrots. There are recipes for making potting soil using peat moss or coconut fiber, perlite or vermiculite, and compost. I assume that ornamental plants have chemical fertilizer in the soil and buy very small plants, gently shake off the soil and repot in my preferred mixture. Access to the soil can be limited in a number of ways, remembering that soil needs air to remain healthy. Well cleaned stones and rocks, a plastic mesh cover placed over the top of the soil are some ideas. Also, plant location (more later) can

keep a parrot out of the dirt. Mold and fungus are dangerous. Appropriately watered plants are not supposed to develop these diseases....but...things happen. One preventative is adding grapefruit seed extract to the water every so often. I water plants with a solution (10-15 drops GSE per gallon) every two or three weeks. If fungus or mold develops, remove the plant from any area in which the parrot will be or is a source of air it will breathe, and destroy or decontaminate the plant and soil. Containers for plants, as with soil, should be made of material that is a "safe chew" or be inaccessible to the curious beak.

Location, location, location is important and will set the parameters, if not dictate, how you approach soil, container and other safety issues. Using plants in a parrot's environment is a type of toy, so: Know your parrot! So far, my parrot gardening presumes supervision, except for a plant that is hung close enough to the cage so a stem or leaf, but not the container, can be nibbled at leisure. Lord Grayson (an African grey) can fly, but his main interest is hanging on his "boing" or sitting on the edge of a pot chewing flowers or greenery. Lady Scarlett (a scarlet macaw) would devour everything in reach, but cannot fly, so I position perches close to the plant parts that can tolerate her pruning. Sometimes though, she is so intent on some morsel just out of her reach that she falls in a pot. I rescue her, wash her off and put her back on the perch. And the little guys can get right in the middle of things!

If you have a bird room or aviary where your parrots are out of their cages without your presence, incorporating plants is a bigger challenge. The principles are the same, but the precautions that need to be taken are much greater. If you have hanging plants, could the bird become tangled in the rope or wire? Do you plan to alternate plants to recover from serious pruning? One idea would be to put the plants in cages, with stems, branches and leaves extending out into the parrot's space. If you have an outdoor aviary, butterfly bush, snowball (viburnum), pussy willow, forsythia or other parrot-safe vigorous hardy bushes could be planted in the aviary. By mid-summer these shrubs always need pruning. Give your birds a job! Grape vines are fun and safe. Tropical plants, hibiscus and palms, for example, can be set out during the summer in large pots in colder climates. Stand a

large clay pipe on end, fill it with soil and add some greens.

REFERENCES AND RESOURCES LISTS OF SAFE AND TOXIC PLANTS:
http://www.birdsnways.com/articles/plntsafe.htm
http://www.birdsnways.com/articles/plntstox.htm
http://www.plannedparrothood.com/plants.html
http://www.exoticbird.com/gillian/plants.html
http://www.holisticbird.org/pages/eplants.htm
http://www.petbirdbreeder.com/safeplants.htm
http://www.petbirdbreeder.com/toxicplants.htm
http://www.avianweb.com/safefoods.html Discussion of use of plants as well as identification of safe and harmful plants:
http://www.landofvos.com/eclectus.html (Kitchen Physician and other articles)
http://exoticedibles.com/ Branches and wood:
http://www.mdvaden.com/bird_page.shtml
http://www.birdsafe.com/woods.htm
http://www.exoticbird.com/gillian/perch.html

Common and scientific names:
http://www.plantsciences.ucdavis.edu/ce/king/PoisPlant/Tox-COM.htm
http://www.bonsai-bci.com/species/common_index.html
http://www.ansci.cornell.edu/plants/index.html
Discussion group of parrot, amphibian, reptile owners:
http://groups.yahoo.com/group/ExoticPetsGardening/
Information about sustainable agriculture, including information on soils:
http://www.attra.ncat.org/ Aviary Resources (a sample of what is out there)
Article about using nylon sports netting:
http://www.parrotchronicles.com/winter2001/feature2.htm
Stainless wire/mesh source: http://www.twpinc.com;
Stainless steel fasteners: www.thenuttycompany.com
Cages By Design: www.cagesbydesign.com
Corners Limited: www.cornerslimited.com
Expandable Habitats: http://www.expandablehabitats.com/custom.htm
Back yard Aviaries: http://birdstheword.com/birds/flight.htm
Discussion group: http://pets.groups.yahoo.com/group/naturalbird/

Section on Aviaries in "Parrot Enrichment and Activity Book," by Kris Porter, www.phoenixlanding.org/PEAB_V2.pdf

Special thanks to Carolyn Swicegood (Land of Vos) and Denise Testa (Exotic Edibles)

CONTAINER GARDENS FOR PARROTS
by Laura Ford

If you don't have the time or the space for a big garden, consider creating a container garden. By choosing a variety of textures and shades of healthy greens, mixing in a few herbs and some edible flowers, you can have a container garden that is delicious, nutritious and beautiful.

Listed below are just a few plants you could choose, along with which parts are edible and their benefits.

Basil – leaves and flowers. Mosquito repellent. Antimicrobial, antibacterial, fungicidal. Soothes itchy skin. Liver decongestant. Balances blood sugar.

Beets – leaves and root. Cleansing to kidneys, regeneration of liver cells, increase oxygen in the blood, support formation of new blood cells, normalize body's pH. Vitamins A and C, niacin, biotin, calcium, iron, magnesium, manganese, phosphorus, potassium, sodium, betaine, betacynin, beta carotene, leucine, tyrosine.

Broccoli – leaves, stem, crowns, flowers. Antioxidant, antibacterial. Vitamins A and C.

Calendula – flowers. Soothing and regenerative to the skin. Anti-inflammatory, astringent, antimicrobial, antifungal, antiviral. Heals wounds, cuts, scrapes, rashes, bee stings, burns, and bruises by stimulating white blood cells. Carotene, iodine, and manganese.

Celery – stalks, leaves, seeds. Supports kidneys, helpful in treatment of gout, rheumatism, and arthritis, tranquilizing, aids in treatment of depression. Vitamins A, C, and B-complex, carotenes, folic acid, potassium, calcium, iron.

Chamomile – flowers, leaves, stems. Soothing to the digestive system. Rejuvenates skin. Decreases feather plucking. Relaxing for nervous birds. Decreases night thrashing.

Cilantro - leaves and stems. Removes heavy metals, lead and aluminum from the body. Antiviral, antibacterial.

Dandelion – leaves, flowers, seeds, root. Detoxifies liver, gall bladder, and blood. Soothes skin irritation. Reduces uric acid.

32, General Information, Tips and Ideas

Antibiotic for lung infections. Beta carotene, vitamins D, B and C, potassium, calcium.

Fennel – leaves, stems, flowers, and seeds. Digestive aid, cold and flu remedy.

Kale – leaves and flowers. Lowers risk of heart disease, stroke, and cataracts, anticancer compounds, immune system stimulant. Vitamins C and E, beta carotene, calcium, potassium, manganese, iron. Among highest sources of chlorophyll.

Mustard Greens – leaves and flowers. Vitamin A and calcium.

Marigolds – flowers. Repels insects. Carotene, Vitamin A. (Lemon Gem and Tangerine Gem have the best flavor, although all varieties are edible.)

Nasturtiums – leaves and flowers. Supports respiratory system

Parsley – leaves and stems. Increases resistance to infections and diseases. Anti-cancer compounds. Blood builder. Vitamins A and C, iron and chlorophyll.

Peppermint – leaves and stems. Stimulates nerves. Oxygen to blood stream. Digestive aid. Vitamins A and C, magnesium, potassium, niacin, copper, iodine, silicon, iron and sulphur.

Plantain – leaves. Antimicrobial, anti-inflammatory, anti hemorrhagic, antitoxic. Promotes healing and cell regeneration. Soothes and softens skin, reducing feather plucking. Soothes respiratory tract. Helps prevent crop infections. Beta carotene, vitamins C and K, calcium.

Pansies, Violas, Violets – leaves and flowers. Soothes itchy skin. Supports and strengthens capillary health. Helps treat and prevent glaucoma.

Peas – stems, leaves, flowers, pods. Vitamin A, phosphorus, thiamin, niacin

Rosemary – leaves and stems. Stimulates circulatory system, strengthening nerves and heart. Anti-cancer compounds. Antibacterial. Soothing to the lungs.

Swiss Chard – leaves. Vitamins A and calcium

RECOMMENDED RESOURCES

What Happened to My Peanuts? by Gudrun Maybaum
Holistic Care For Birds by David McCluggage, DVM and Pamela Leis Higdon
The Green Pharmacy by James A Duke, PhD
Edible Flowers, From Garden To Palate by Cathy Wilkinson Barash
Flowers in the Kitchen by Susan Belisinger
Herbs for Health, periodical, February 2008
Mother Earth News, periodical, July 1983
Celebirds.com

VEGETABLE SECTION

- Butternut Squash "Gratin"   Page 36
- Carrot Risotto   Page 36
- Pumpkin Bread   Page 37
- Pumpkin Cookies   Page 37
- Another Birdie Bread   Page 38
- Pumpkin Pancakes or Bread   Page 38
- Vegetable Ravioli   Page 39
- The Layered Fresh Food Mix   Page 40
- Pumpkin Pie Lasagna   Page 44
- Pumpkin Groats With Turkey   Page 44
- Broccoli Slaw   Page 45
- Lentil Carrot Burgers   Page 45
- Vegetable Nut Pate   Page 45
- Pumpkin Hula   Page 46
- Baked And Stuffed Pumpkin   Page 46
- Crunchy Pumpkin Salad   Page 46
- Carrot, Nuts And Rice Burgers   Page 47
- Pumpkin Ambrosia   Page 47
- Roasted Pumpkin Seeds   Page 48
- Pumpkin Stuffed Peppers   Page 48
- Corn, Zucchini And Tomatoes   Page 48
- Kale-Quinoa Salad With Cherries And Almonds   Page 49
- Vegetables With Vinaigrette   Page 49
- George's Sweet Potato Flax Seed Bread   Page 50
- Veggies, Nuts, And Yogurt   Page 50
- Vegetables And Quinoa Pasta   Page 51
- Mashed Sweet Potatoes With Coconut Milk   Page 51
- Couscous Carrots and Cranberries   Page 51
- Sweet Potato Fries #1-2   Page 52
- Sweet Potato Fries #3-4   Page 53
- Trixie's Sweet Potato Fries   Page 53
- Tropical Sweet Potatoes   Page 54
- Pumpkin Cranberry Bread   Page 54
- Vegetable And Rice Stuffed Pumpkin   Page 55
- Kale Casserole   Page 56
- Veggie Rice And Garbanzos With Coconut   Page 56
- Veggie Patties   Page 57

34, Vegetables

- Vegetable Brown Rice — Page 57
- Parker's Perfect Potpourri — Page 58
- Vegetable Couscous — Page 59
- Thyme Carrots — Page 59
- Birdie Baked Taters — Page 60
- Carrot Patties — Page 60
- Pumpkin Seed And Carrot Patties — Page 61
- Carrot And Oatmeal Cookies — Page 61
- Sweet Potato And Banana Crunch — Page 62
- Sweet Potato Puffs — Page 62
- Carrot Spread — Page 62
- Sweet Potato Falafel — Page 63
- Sauteed Veggies and Garbanzos — Page 63
- Sweet Potato Casserole — Page 64
- Ginger Cumin Carrots — Page 64
- Curry Coconut Butternut Squash — Page 64
- Baked And Stuffed Acorn Squash — Page 65
- Greens and Cranberries — Page 65
- Pineapple Greens with Peanut Butter — Page 65
- Chop Chop! — Page 66-67

Vegetables are one of the most important food sources for your parrot, containing a wide variety of nutrients. Many of the recipes in this book involve cooked foods, but chopping raw veggies is equally good or better! Cut the produce to a size that best suits your parrot.

Large birds enjoy may holding chunks, small birds may want their foods cut into smaller pieces. If your bird does not eat a wide variety, puree the veggies into a mash texture and sprinkle with a favorite "condiment" like nuts or granola. Over time you can reduce the quantity of the condiment, or make the mash chunkier. If you use organic produce, let your bird do the peeling! Include in your bird's diet as many leafy greens and foods with beta-carotene as possible.

Make sure any warm foods are sufficiently cool before serving.

Vegetables, 35

BUTTERNUT SQUASH "GRATIN"
by Leigh Ann Hartsfield

- 3 cups butternut squash (about ½ a squash) seeded and sliced into chunks Reserve seeds for another purpose.
- 1 cup "Minute" brown rice
- 1 jar baby food-like Gerber's Organic Turkey, Vegetables, and Barley
- Wholegrain bread-like Arnold's 12 Grain

Steam squash until soft, about 12-15 minutes. Meanwhile, prepare rice following instructions on box. Remove peel from softened squash, if desired. Blend squash in food processor or blender until smooth. Add jar of baby food and continue to blend until a soft puree consistency is reached. Stir in brown rice.

Just before serving, toast a slice of the bread. Using a dry food processor, chop toast until you have crunchy bread crumbs. Add to rice and squash mixture. (Note: It is important that the food processor be clean and dry before making the bread crumbs; otherwise, they'll be soggy. The crunchy texture is appealing to most parrots.) If freezing or refrigerating unused portions, consider adding fresh crunchy bread crumbs to each meal served.

CARROT RISOTTO

- ¾ cup brown rice
- 1 ½ cups water
- 4 large carrots
- Small amount of shredded Parmesan cheese

Bring the water and brown rice to a boil, then turn to a simmer and cover for 45-50 minutes, until cooked.

Cut unpeeled carrots into ½-inch pieces and steam until just tender, about 10 minutes. Reserve the water, and puree cooked carrots in a food processor until smooth. Add spoonfuls of cooking water as needed to thin the puree to the consistency of applesauce.

Combine carrot puree and rice. Sprinkle with a small amount of Parmesan cheese or other favorite condiments.

PUMPKIN BREAD

A birdie bread without the wheat! Every ingredient is healthy.

- 1 egg
- Small 15-oz can of organic pumpkin
- Teaspoon pumpkin pie spice (or pumpkin with spice already included)
- ½ cup yogurt
- 2 cups oatmeal ground up into flour *
- ½ cup ground nuts and unsulfured dried fruits
- 2 heaping tablespoons of organic applesauce, any flavor (an oil substitute)

Stir all ingredients together.   Yogurt is optional. Scoop out into a cast iron skillet. Bake at 350 until completely cooked through, about 40 minutes. Use a toothpick to test doneness. You can also form into balls or make cookies with this batter, if preferred.

This recipe is a big hit with almost all birds, and pumpkin is a very good source of vitamin A. Just remember to make EVERY ingredient a healthy one, and avoid those quick mix cornbread products!!

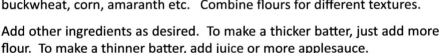

* Substitute other flours such as garbanzo bean, wheat, quinoa, coconut, buckwheat, corn, amaranth etc.   Combine flours for different textures.

Add other ingredients as desired. To make a thicker batter, just add more flour. To make a thinner batter, add juice or more applesauce.

PUMPKIN COOKIES

- 2 cups flour
- 1 cup old fashioned oats, uncooked
- 1 teaspoon cinnamon
- 1 cup applesauce
- 1 egg slightly beaten
- 1 teaspoon vanilla
- 1 cup pumpkin

Preheat oven to 350 degrees. Combine flour, oats and cinnamon. Mix eggs and vanilla. Alternate addition of dry ingredients and pumpkin, mixing well after each addition. Drop by teaspoons, on lightly greased cookie sheet. Bake 8 – 10 minutes until lightly browned.

Vegetables, 37

ANOTHER BIRDIE BREAD
by Elizabeth Bouldin-Clopton

- 1 cup almond flour, 4 ounces
- ¾ cup hazelnut flour, about 3 ounces
- ¼ cup soy grits, about 1 ¾ ounces
- 1 cup corn grits or stone-ground corn meal
- ½ cup golden flax
- ½ cup whole wheat flour
- ½ cup rolled oats or steel cut oats
- 2 teaspoons baking powder
- 1 15-ounce can solid pack pumpkin
- ⅓ cup olive or canola oil
- 4 eggs, shell included (organic if using shells!)
- 1 cored apple
- 1 ½ cups orange, apple, papaya, pineapple or other fruit juice
- ½ bell pepper, seeds included
- Assorted other vegetables - up to two cups - broccoli, squash, peppers, spinach (a good way to get greens in)
- ½ cup shredded coconut
- ¼ cup currants or raisins, diced prunes or diced dates

Put the eggs, apple, juice, pepper and veggies in the blender and blend on high until liquid. Pour into a bowl and add the oil and pumpkin. Stir in the dry ingredients. If the mixture is too dry, add more juice until the consistency is like banana bread or thick cake mix. Pour into 9x13" pan and bake at 325 for 45-50 minutes. If the consistency after baking is still sticky, cut it into cubes and bake them on a cookie sheet for 10-15 minutes.

This recipe is high protein, includes a lot of delicious things birds like and provides a lot of nutrition.

PUMPKIN PANCAKES OR BREAD

- 4 eggs
- 1 container of cottage cheese (1 lb)
- 1 15-oz can of pumpkin puree, can include pie spices
- 2 cups flour (garbanzo, ground oatmeal, wheat)
- 4-oz small container of applesauce

Blend eggs, cottage cheese and pumpkin in a blender until smooth and add other ingredients. Bake on lightly greased griddle. Make a few pancakes for yourself and the birds, and then put the rest in a cast iron skillet and make the batter into a delightful birdie bread. Bake at 350 degrees for 35 minutes.

VEGETABLE RAVIOLI
by Kris Porter

- 2 cups whole grain flour
- ½ cup carrot or other vegetable juice warmed to about 70 to 80 degrees

1. Place flour in a large bowl. Add warm juice and stir to make a stiff dough. Increase juice if dough seems too dry.
2. Pat the dough into a ball and turn out onto a lightly floured surface. Knead for 10 to 15 minutes. Cover with a damp cloth. Let dough rest for 20 minutes.
3. Roll out dough using rolling pin or pasta machine. Work with ¼ of the dough at one time. Keep the rest covered, to prevent from drying out. Roll by hand to 1/16 of an inch thick. By machine, stop at the third to last setting.
4. Cut pasta into large strips (about 1 inch wide).
5. Place small amount of a veggie paste about ¼ inch from edge of strip. Fold over and cut off. Crimp edges of the ravioli. (I use a pastry wheel to cut the strips and also crimp the edges)
6. Cook fresh pasta in boiling water for 5 to 6 minutes. Drain.
7. Add pasta sauce and let cool a bit before serving to the birds.

VEGGIE PASTE: Cook and mash 1 yam. To the mashed yam add finely chopped vegetables such as; turnip, collard or mustard greens; broccoli, or any vegetables you use to feed the parrots. I make concentrated veggie pastes and freeze them to add to recipes as I need them.

PASTA SAUCE: Make a thick pasta sauce of cooked pureed vegetables. For the recipe pictured, I cooked and pureed butternut squash with a small amount of broccoli and collard greens. To the vegetable puree I added ground almonds and water until I had the consistency that would stick to the pasta. (Instead of making your own puree; you could substitute organic baby food)

* I have a Vita-Mix with a dry blade container that grinds grains, beans and rice to make nutrient-dense flour. For the flour in this recipe I used equal parts lentil, quinoa, spelt, kamut, buckwheat and oat groats. If you don't have equipment to grind your own flour, you can purchase whole grain flours in the bulk food section of the grocery store and make your own flour mix. Often you can find garbanzo bean, quinoa, buckwheat and barley flours. Some natural food stores will grind whole grain for you.

NOTE: The ravioli can also be frozen for use later. Place them in a single layer on a cookie sheet lined with parchment or wax paper. When frozen, place in baggies and store in freezer until later. Frozen pasta will need to boil for about 8 to 10 minutes.

THE LAYERED FRESH FOOD MIX
by Pamela Clark, CVT

This diet has several advantages, not the least of which is that I can feed fresh foods to any number of parrots, while only chopping fruits and vegetables once a week. I originally learned this method from Jamie McLeod in Summerland, California and have modified it through the years.

Once a week, prepare a layered salad mix as follows, and place this into individual plastic containers. For one parrot, you might make three quart-sized containers. For 10 parrots, you might make four gallon-sized containers. For 30 parrots, you might make seven two-gallon containers. It may take some playing around with this before you find the right combination of numbers and sizes of containers to create just enough layered salad to last for 7 days.

Lay out your containers and wash your fruits and vegetables thoroughly, drying them before use. Greens should be dried in a salad spinner. To wash vegetables use the Oxyfresh Cleaning Gele or any vegetable wash sold for that purpose.

After washing and drying, chop and place into your containers the fruits and vegetables as indicated below:

Layer 1 (bottom layer) - chopped greens, which are varied each week. Options include collard greens, parsley, mustard greens, Swiss chard, kale and dandelion greens. (If you have only one parrot, or a few parrots, just choose one type of greens, but vary this weekly.)

Layer 2 - chopped (¼ to ½ inch cubes) vegetables, including any of the following: Brussels sprouts, zucchini and other summer squash, jicama, red or green peppers, fresh hot peppers, chayote squash, green beans, fresh peas, cucumber, celery, anise root, etc. If making this for only one to three parrots, you will find that the amount of variety you can include each week in this layer will be limited. Try to include at least five different vegetables in this layer and alternate these each week.

Layer 3 - chopped broccoli and carrots

Layer 4 - a mixture of chopped apples, oranges and whole grapes

Layer 5 - frozen mixed vegetables.

The containers are then covered tightly and placed in the refrigerator (don't freeze).

Issues of freshness: this mix stays fresh in these tubs for up to seven days for three reasons. First, layered salads stay fresher longer. Second, the orange juice from the chopped oranges filters down and slightly acidifies the mix. Third, the frozen mixed vegetables placed on top super-cool the mix immediately. Lastly, the ingredients have been well-washed and dried to exclude excess moisture.

Use: Each morning or as often as you need to, empty out one container into a large mixing bowl, and add other items that would not hold up or stay fresh in the layered mix. Staple items to add each time:

Cooked beans
You can cook a combination of dried beans, then freeze these in appropriately-sized baggies to defrost prior to adding to the mix.
• To cook dried beans, soak these overnight in water to cover. Drain them and rinse them thoroughly the next morning. Then, cover them again with fresh water, bring to a full boil and simmer for 15 minutes. Allow to cool, then drain and freeze.
• If creating this mix for one to three parrots, freeze beans in snack-sized baggies. If creating this mix for three to seven parrots, use sandwich-sized baggies. If creating this mix for over seven to 12 parrots, use quart-sized baggies.
You can also simply add canned beans. If you choose this option, vary the type you add from week to week to increase variety.

Cooked grains
• A rice cooker is a wonderful appliance for parrot owners. Any grain can be easily and quickly cooked in a rice cooker. Grains to purchase from your local health food store include: quinoa, brown rice, oat groats, wheat berries, hulled barley, and rye berries.
• These can be cooked individually or in combination with each other and then frozen in similar fashion to the beans, in the same quantities indicated above.
• Adding cooked beans and grains together in the salad is important, since their combination will provide a protein source.

Fruit
Other fruit in season (blueberries, peaches, plums, kiwi fruits, cranberries, melon, etc).
• A small amount of a high-quality, clean seed mix – this should make up no more than 5% of the total mix when finished.

Other items that can be added occasionally for variety include:
• Sprouts
I purchase seeds from my health food store and make my own mix, which

Vegetables, 41

includes: shelled, raw sunflower seeds, raw buckwheat, French green lentils, sesame seeds, wheat berries, hulled barley, rye berries, and mung beans. These are all about the same size, so sprout at the same time.

I also occasionally sprout garbanzo beans and popcorn, both of which require a longer sprouting time.

The best sprouting equipment is the "Easy-Sprout" system, which can be ordered from www.sproutamo.com.

- Uncooked whole wheat pasta
- Flax seeds
- A sprinkle of pine nuts or walnut pieces
- Firm tofu, diced into squares
- Corn on the cob slices, quartered
- Cooked and diced beets
- Dried goji berries (available from the health food store and high in nutritional value)
- Scenic Diet Hand Weaning pellets or other pelleted diet (This can be a successful way to introduce pellets to a parrot who won't eat them.)

Once everything is mixed together, the salad is ready for feeding. I feed a level cup of this to each parrot, along with some type of "extra" – perhaps a nut in the shell or a piece of birdie bread. The remainder of the mix is then placed back into the container and refrigerated for the next feeding. Once mixed together in this way, the salad should be used completely within one to two days. I arrange things so that one tub, after mixing, will be used for three feedings. Since I feed this two times a day, each tub then lasts a day and a half. Don't be tempted to use a mix longer than two days because it will not stay fresh longer than this.

This recipe can be adapted for any number of birds with a little creativity, by changing either the number or size of the containers used or both. It may take some playing around to find the right-sized containers, as well as the right amount of veggies and fruits to include, in terms of variety – but it will be well worth it. I promise you!

Feeding this salad has several advantages:
- It includes a variety of live, raw foods that provide nutrients that are usually destroyed when foods are processed or cooked.
- There's no need to chop fresh fruits and vegetables every day.
- The mixture maintains a similar uniform appearance, no matter what you put into it. This helps with the introduction of seasonal foods, such as blueberries that a parrot might otherwise reject simply because they aren't visually familiar with them.
- A huge amount of variety can be achieved. The types of vegetables

and greens can be varied each week. Vary the pasta shapes. Substitute other types of citrus for the oranges. Use different types of seed mixes.

• This mix is exciting for our parrots, and allows them a true foraging experience. By always seeking to include a wide variety of foods in this mix, we cultivate in them a joy and excitement about eating. It helps to foster great eating habits.

• Further, if well-prepared, this mix can be left in the cage for several hours, which isn't true for cooked foods.

• And lastly, seed junkies can easily by converted to a fresh food diet using this mix and a methodical approach, which I have outlined below.

Diet Conversion

1. Begin with four dishes in the cage – (1) pellets of choice (no dyes or preservatives hopefully), (2) a high quality seed mix, (3) water and (4) the fresh food mix into which you have mixed seed. The latter may not be eaten for several weeks. Don't be discouraged by this. Serve the fresh food mix twice a day, in the morning and in the late afternoon or evening, for the sole purpose of creating a pattern of feeding and allowing the bird to get used to looking at it. Note: the fresh food mix should have a ratio of 50% seed and 50% fresh foods from the recipe above (pellets optional). Try not to provide table food or "treats" between these two feeding times.

2. The day you see the bird exploring the fresh food mix in order to eat the seed out of it, you make the following change: In the morning, you remove the seed dish and have only three dishes in the cage – (1) pellets, (2) water and (3) the fresh mix. In the evening, you again feed the fresh food mix, but give the seed dish back. We don't want a bird undergoing diet conversion to be hungry. A hungry, anxious bird does not make behavioral changes gracefully.

3. The day you see the bird with a piece of fresh food in his mouth, or observe that he has eaten some of it, you eliminate the seed dish completely from his cage and from this point onward you won't be feeding seed at all, except as part of the fresh food mix. From that point onward, you provide only three dishes – (1) water, (2) pellets, and (3) the fresh mix that is 50% seed and 50% fresh foods.

4. A month later, and on each succeeding month, you decrease the amount of seed in the mix until it is down to only 5 % of the mix. So, for instance, if you remove the seed dish on February 1, then on March 1, you will begin to feed a mix that is 40% seed and 60% fresh mix. On April 1, you will begin to feed 30% seed and 70% fresh foods. And so on.

Vegetables, 43

PUMPKIN PIE LASAGNA

- 5 cups of veggies, shredded or chopped. If organic, leave the peels!
- (A suggestion: small stalk broccoli, ½ sweet potato or winter squash, 2 carrots, 2 stalks kale)
- 1 cup unsulfured dried fruit (papaya, cranberries, cherries..)
- 1 ½ cups grain PASTA (quinoa, kamut etc), cooked or uncooked per your bird's preference

Put the layer of pasta on the bottom of a 8" square baking dish. Stir veggies and fruit together and spoon over the pasta.

Mix together a can of organic PUMPKIN pie mix (15 oz.), 2 eggs, ½ cup pure JUICE (no sugar or additives). Blend together. Pour over veggie/fruit mix, spooning it between the chunks. Top with chopped walnuts or brazil NUTS.

Cook at 425 for 15 minutes. Reduce to 350 for 30 minutes, or until the pumpkin is cooked.

Top some chopped chicken or fish, pineapple chunks, or alfalfa sprinkles. Be creative!

PUMPKIN GROATS with TURKEY

- 4 cups liquid (combination of sodium free chicken or vegetable broth, pure juice or water)
- 1 tablespoon coconut oil
- 1 cup buckwheat groats
- 1 teaspoon cinnamon
- ½ teaspoon ginger
- ⅓ pound ground turkey
- 1 cup canned pumpkin puree or pumpkin pie mix

In a small pot, warm the chicken broth over low heat.
In a large skillet, melt the coconut oil over medium heat, then add the groats and toast for 3-4 minutes, stirring occasionally. Season the grains with the cinnamon and stir in half of the warm broth. Cook until the broth bubbles, about 5 minutes. Then add the turkey, crumbling it as you drop it into the skillet, and cook until the liquid is absorbed by the grains, about 5 minutes. Stir in the remaining broth, ½ cup at a time, allowing the broth to be fully absorbed before adding more. Cook until the groats are tender, about 18 minutes. Stir in the pumpkin puree. Cook over medium heat until just heated through, about 1 minute.

BROCCOLI SLAW

- 4 broccoli stems, washed
- 6-inch piece of daikon radish (no need to peel)
- 2 large carrots (no need to peel)
- 2 kiwis, peeled and diced
- 3 TBL pine nuts, toasted or raw
- 2 cloves garlic, minced
- Flax seed oil
- Unhulled sesame seeds

Coarsely grate broccoli stems, daikon radish, and carrots according to your parrot's preferences and put into a bowl. Add kiwis, pine nuts, and garlic to bowl and toss together. Drizzle flax oil or stir in some palm oil. Garnish with a generous sprinkling of unhulled sesame seeds.

LENTIL CARROT BURGERS

- 1 cup grated carrots
- ½ cup pure juice (mango, carrot, pineapple..)
- 2 cups cooked lentils, mashed
- ¾ cups bread crumbs, made from toasted whole grain bread

Cook the carrots in the juice until tender, about 10 minutes. Drain and combine with the lentils and bread crumbs. Mix well and create patties. Cook on a cookie sheet at 350 degrees, about 10 minutes on each side.

Variations: try sweet potatoes instead of carrots; add cooked brown rice; add spices like cumin, thyme or rosemary. Or, add all to a baking dish for 20 minutes and top with a small amount of cheddar cheese. Be creative!

VEGETABLE NUT PATE

- 1 cup steamed vegetables (carrots, green beans, sweet potatoes, squash, broccoli)
- ½ cup chopped brazil or walnuts

Steam vegetables for about 10 minutes. Place vegetables and nuts in a food processor and puree until smooth. Serve on rice cakes or a piece of whole grain toast.

Walnuts have a high concentration of the important Omega-3 fatty acid. 15% of the fat found in walnuts is healthful monounsaturated fat. Walnuts are a particularly good addition to macaw diets, and they can enjoy about 6 whole walnuts a day. Let them do the cracking!

Vegetables, 45

PUMPKIN HULA

- 1-2 oranges, peeled and thinly sliced
- 1 can organic pumpkin, add 1 TBL pumpkin pie spice
- 1 small can crushed pineapple, WELL DRAINED
- Shredded coconut

Thinly slice the orange. Alternate layers of orange and pumpkin in baking dish. Top with pineapple. Sprinkle coconut on top. Also nice addition to the topping would be slivered almonds and unhulled sesame seeds. Bake at 350 degrees for 30-40 minutes. Cool before serving.

BAKED and STUFFED PUMPKIN

- 2 pound pumpkin, washed
- 2 apples, cored, quartered
- ½ cup pineapple chunks
- ½ cup broken walnuts
- 1 teaspoon ground cinnamon
- ¼ teaspoon ground cloves

Cut a wide top off the pumpkin and remove the seeds. Place cut side down in a baking pan and bake at 350 degrees for about 40 minutes or until soft. Cool.

With a metal spoon, scrape out the cooked pumpkin, leaving a ⅛ to ¼ inch thick shell. Process the apples in a food processor until chunky. Add pineapple, walnuts, cinnamon, and cloves and process until just mixed.

Some birds will have fun if the mixture is spooned back into the pumpkin shell, and placed into a bowl.

CRUNCHY PUMPKIN SALAD

- 1 cup chopped cauliflower
- ½ cup chopped celery
- 1 tart apple, chopped
- 1 cup grated raw pumpkin
- 1 cup chopped walnuts
- 1 TBL fresh orange juice
- 1 cup sprouts

Mix together. If storing for use in next day or two, add walnuts and sprouts just before serving.

CARROT, NUTS and RICE BURGERS

- 1 ½ cups uncooked brown rice
- 3 cups water and/or pure carrot juice
- ½ cup toasted unsalted cashews
- ½ pound toasted unsalted, unshelled sunflower seeds
- 3 carrots, shredded
- ½ cup raw pumpkin seeds
- Coconut oil for grilling

In a large pan, bring the rice and water to a boil. Reduce heat to low, cover, and simmer 50 minutes.

Grind the toasted cashews and sunflower seeds to a fine meal in a food processor. Transfer to a large bowl. Pulse the carrots in a food processor until finely shredded, and mix with the ground nuts. Place the cooked rice in the food processor and pulse until smooth. Mix into the bowl. Add pumpkin seeds. Stir well. Form the mixture into patties.

Grill the patties in a bit more coconut oil for 6 to 8 minutes on each side, until nicely browned.

We don't recommend sunflower seeds as a significant portion of a bird's diet; however, this recipe might be enticing to some birds for this reason, and be a good way to get them started towards fresh foods. These burgers are very dense, so feed only as a small proportion of a meal, similar to birdie bread.

PUMPKIN AMBROSIA

- 1 peeled orange cut in segments
- 1 tart apple, chopped
- 1 cup grated raw pumpkin
- 1 cup flaked or shredded coconut
- 1 cup yogurt

Mix together. If storing, squeeze 1 teaspoon of lemon juice and wait to add yogurt until just before serving.

ROASTED PUMPKIN SEEDS

- Scoop out the seeds from the pumpkin
- Separate and discard pulp
- Wash seeds in warm water
- Spread seeds onto a cookie sheet
- Bake at 350 degrees for approximately 20 minutes
- Check every five minutes and stir
- Check seeds to see if they are done by taking a sample out, allowing to cool and tasting. If the insides are dry, they are done
- Allow to cool and serve

PUMPKIN STUFFED PEPPERS

- 2 peppers (green, red, yellow or orange)
- 1 small clove of garlic
- ¼ pound of ground chicken or turkey
- ¼ cup grated, raw pumpkin
- 1 slice of whole grain bread, ground

Parboil peppers for 3 minutes. Cool and cut in half, lengthwise. Mix cooked meat, garlic and pumpkin together. Make bread crumbs and add to mixture. Fill pepper shells. Bake for 30-40 minutes at 350 degrees.

CORN, ZUCCHINI and TOMATOES

- 2 tablespoons coconut oil
- 3 medium zucchini, cut into ½ inch slices (or as preferred by your bird's size)
- 1 package frozen organic corn, defrosted
- 1 teaspoon oregano, fresh if possible
- 2 ½ pounds plum tomatoes, chopped (or use 28-ounce can organic plum tomatoes)

Heat coconut oil in skillet over medium heat. Stir in zucchini. Stir and cook for a minute. Stir in remaining ingredients, breaking up the tomatoes, heat to boiling, reduce heat. Cover and simmer about 15 minutes or until the zucchini is tender. Sprinkle a small bit of Parmesan cheese for birds that need an incentive, or other condiments as desired.

KALE-QUINOA SALAD with CHERRIES and ALMONDS

- ¼ cup sliced almonds
- 1 ½ cups quinoa, rinsed and drained
- 2 cups kale
- 2 cups fresh cherries, pitted and halved; or 1 cup dried cherries, chopped
- 1 cucumber, peeled, and cut into 1/3-inch dice (about 1 ½ cups)
- 1 15-oz can chickpeas, rinsed and drained
- ¼ cup plain low-fat yogurt
- 1 TBL. fresh lemon juice
- 2 cloves garlic, minced

Preheat oven to 350 degrees. Spread almonds on baking sheet, and toast 7 to 10 minutes, shaking pan occasionally, or until golden brown. Cool.

Bring 3 cups water to a boil in pot over medium-high heat. Stir in quinoa. Reduce heat to medium low, cover, and simmer 10-15 minutes, or until the quinoa blossoms. Remove from heat and cool. Drain any excess liquid.

Lay kale leaves flat on top of one another on cutting board. Roll tightly into cylinder, then slice into slivers.

Toss together almonds, quinoa, kale, cherries, cucumber, and chickpeas in large serving bowl. Whisk together yogurt, lemon juice and garlic in a small bowl. Pour over salad, and toss to coat. Can be served immediately, or chill for 30 minutes. Only pour the yogurt dressing for the portions that will be eaten that day. Humans may want to add some olive oil, salt and pepper in their portion.

VEGETABLES WITH VINAIGRETTE
by Gudrun Maybaum, www.totallyorganics.com

This recipe can be done with spinach, zucchini, chard, etc.

- Vegetables
- Olive oil
- Fresh pressed lemon juice

Cook vegetables, best in steam, but still a little crisp

Mix about 4 tablespoons of olive oil with half as much lemon juice. Whisk until it is kind of foamy, add to the vegetables, mix well. Ready to eat.

Vegetables, 49

GEORGE'S SWEET POTATO FLAX SEED BREAD
by Kathleen O'Neill

This recipe is adapted from a Cooking Lite recipe so it is good and healthy for birds and people.

- ⅓ cup flax seed
- 1 cup all purpose flour
- 1 cup whole wheat flour
- 1 teaspoon baking powder
- ½ teaspoon baking soda
- ¼ cup yogurt
- 3 tablespoons softened butter
- ¼ cup honey
- ¼ cup brown sugar
- 1 large egg
- 1 large egg white
- 1 ½ cups mashed cooked sweet potato

Preheat oven to 350 degrees. Place flaxseed in a grinder or blender and process until coarsely ground. Combine flaxseed, flour, baking powder, and baking soda in a large bowl. In a separate bowl beat yogurt, butter, sugar, honey and eggs, stir in sweet potato. Add to the flour mixture and stir just until moist.

Spoon batter into a greased 8 x 4 inch loaf pan and bake at 350 for 50 minutes or until a toothpick inserted into the center comes out clean.

[If just for the birds, the brown sugar is not needed and 3 TBL of applesauce can be substituted for the butter. With those ingredients, use for treats only.]

VEGGIES, NUTS, and YOGURT
by Megan Burnham-Gerow

A quick, easy recipe. No measuring, no thinking, just toss together.

- Shred / grate your bird's favorite veggies
- Add a couple of sliced grapes
- Some chopped walnuts, almonds or whatever other nuts they like
- Mix together with plain, non-fat yogurt
- Feed!

(Don't leave in the cage all day because of the yogurt)

VEGETABLES and QUINOA PASTA

- 2 TBLs walnut oil (or coconut oil)
- 4-oz quinoa pasta (or other healthy versions like kamut or gluten free)
- 1 small red bell pepper, cut in thin strips or diced
- 2 medium carrots cut in very thin sticks or diced
- 1½ cup zucchini or summer yellow squash, strips or diced
- ¼ cup pasta broth

Bring water to a boil for pasta. Cook pasta, according to package instructions and strain through colander. While pasta is cooking, chop vegetables. Heat 2 TBLs walnut or coconut oil in medium skillet. Add vegetables, one at a time, waiting a couple of minutes between each. Stir so that the oil is tossed with the vegetables. After the last vegetable is added, stir in ¼ cup of the liquid from the cooking pasta, and cover. Simmer until vegetables are barely tender, about 4 minutes. If needed, add a touch more liquid to keep moist. Toss pasta with vegetables. Sprinkle with your bird's favorite condiment such as chicken chunks, pumpkin seeds or unhulled sesame seeds.

MASHED SWEET POTATOES with COCONUT MILK

- 3 large sweet potatoes or yams
- (1) 14 ounce can coconut milk
- 2 teaspoon ginger

Cut the sweet potatoes into 1" chunks, cover in water and bring to a boil. Reduce heat and simmer for at least 15 minutes, or until soft. Mash or use a mixer to blend the sweet potatoes to desired consistency. Add coconut milk and ginger. Some parrots might enjoy a touch of curry or cinnamon. Sprinkle with other favorite condiments as desired. Can be frozen in portions for use later.

COUSCOUS CARROTS and CRANBERRIES

Bring 2 cups of water to a boil. Add some fresh cranberries and 1 cup of shredded carrots. Cook for 5 minutes or less. Add 1/2 cup French couscous. Cook on high for 1 minute. Turn off heat and cover for 5 minutes or so. Drain. Top with other favorites like a sprinkle of cinnamon, chopped walnuts, chicken chunks or pumpkin seeds.

SWEET POTATO FRIES #1

- 1 large organic sweet potato, unpeeled and cut into wedges or cubes
- 2 teaspoons coconut oil, melted
- Pinch of cayenne pepper

Preheat oven to 450 degrees. Toss sweet potato with oil. Spread the wedges on a rimmed baking sheet. Bake until browned and tender, turning once, about 20 minutes total.

SWEET POTATO FRIES #2
by Chris Fleming

Serves: 3-4 people (or several birds!)
Prep time: 5 minutes
Total time: 1 hour

- 3 large sweet potatoes (approximately 2.5 pounds)
- 2-3 tablespoons canola oil
- 2 teaspoons paprika or to taste
- For people: Coarse salt and ground pepper

1. Preheat oven to 450°. Cut potatoes into 1-inch-wide wedges. Toss potatoes with oil and paprika (or other spices); season with salt and pepper for people. Transfer to a rimmed baking sheet.

2. Bake potatoes in a single layer, cut sides down, until they loosen easily from the sheet, about 25 minutes. Turn the potatoes; continue to bake them until fork-tender and crisp, 25 to 30 minutes more.

--- Notes ---
- Use all organic whenever possible.
- Cool before serving to birds - these are very hot out of the oven!! Split open to cool faster.
- I also spice these with other things, including: powdered garlic, cayenne pepper, cinnamon, etc.
- Some people like these served warm with a pat of butter.
- Can also be made in smaller (1 potato) batches.

SWEET POTATO FRIES #3

- 1 large organic sweet potato, unpeeled and cut into 1-inch cubes
- ¼ cup extra-virgin olive oil, plus more for drizzling potatoes after cooked
- ¼ cup honey
- 2 teaspoons ground cinnamon

Preheat oven to 375 degrees. Lay the sweet potatoes out in a single layer on a roasting tray. Combine the oil, honey, and cinnamon. Drizzle over the potatoes. Roast for 25 to 30 minutes in oven or until tender.

SWEET POTATO FRIES #4

Preheat oven to 425 degrees. Cut one large sweet potato into strips. Rinse in water and shake in a bag with a mixture of organic cornmeal flour and a shake of cayenne. Bake on a cookie sheet for 30 minutes, turning over halfway through.

TRIXIE'S SWEET POTATO FRIES
by Laura Ford

- Scrub & dry sweet potatoes
- Cut into desired French fry sized sticks (or can be sliced into "chips")
- Warm about a tablespoon of coconut oil to liquid state
- Toss sweet potatoes in coconut oil to lightly coat
- Spread in a single layer on a cookie sheet
- Sprinkle with cinnamon and cayenne pepper
- Bake in a preheated 400 degree oven for approximately 20 minutes, or until the edges begin to brown

Sweet potatoes are wholesome and easy. Simply steaming chunks as a portion of a meal is easy and really good for your bird. Cook extra and refrigerate 2 or 3 days worth. Freeze the remainder to use as needed. Sweet potatoes can also be blended into a puree, add some favorites to the mix. Beware of microwaving potatoes, as they hold heat and may have hot spots.

Vegetables, 53

TROPICAL SWEET POTATOES

- 3 sweet potatoes, cleaned and pricked all over with a fork
- 1 (8-oz) can crushed organic pineapple, drained
- 1 tablespoons fresh ginger root, minced
- 3 tablespoons unsweetened coconut
- 1 ½ teaspoons orange zest

Cook potatoes in a 400 degree oven until they are soft when squeezed, 45 minutes to 1 hour. Do not overcook -- you want your potatoes tender, but not mushy. Turn down oven heat to 350 degrees.

Cut potatoes in half, lengthwise. Scoop out the potato and place in a medium bowl, being careful not to tear the skin.

Add pineapple, ginger, coconut, and orange zest to the potato. Mash until slightly fluffy.

Place potato skins on a baking sheet. Fill with potato mixture. Bake 15 minutes.

PUMPKIN CRANBERRY BREAD

- 2 ¼ cups flour
- 5/8 teaspoon ginger
- ¼ teaspoon cloves
- 1 ½ teaspoon cinnamon
- 2 beaten eggs
- 1 cup applesauce
- 1 cup pumpkin
- 1 cup chopped cranberries
- ½ cup chopped walnuts

In a large bowl, combine flour and spices. Add applesauce and pumpkin to eggs; beat thoroughly. Add pumpkin mixture to dry ingredients; stir just until moistened. Stir in cranberries and walnuts. Spoon batter into 1 large cast iron skillet, 2 lightly oiled loaf pans, or muffins. Bake at 350° for 50-60 minutes or until toothpick comes out clean. Cool before serving to the birds.

VEGETABLE AND RICE STUFFED PUMPKIN

- 1 pumpkin (14 or 15 inches in diameter) or 2 smaller ones
- 1 cup water
- ¼ cup raisins
- ¼ cup apricots, chopped
- 1 granny smith apple, chopped
- ½ cup walnuts, broken
- 1 stalk celery, chopped
- 1 can corn, drained
- 1 medium green pepper, chopped
- 1 medium red pepper, chopped
- 1 medium zucchini, chopped
- 1 medium yellow squash, chopped
- 2 medium jalapeno peppers, seeded and minced
- 2 cup COOKED brown rice
- ¼ teaspoon mace
- ¼ teaspoon turmeric
- ½ teaspoon cinnamon

1. Preheat oven to 350 degrees. Wash pumpkin and cut off the top, angle the cut so that the top will fit back on more easily, use a big spoon to scoop out strings and seeds. Line the bottom of a large pan with single piece of aluminum foil folded 3 or 4 times, pour 1 cup water in pan, place top back on pumpkin and place in baking pan, cover the pumpkin and the pan with foil. Bake for 20 to 25 minutes until pumpkin is just starting to become tender, the thicker the pumpkin the longer it will take.

2. Combine the raisins, apricots, apple, walnuts, corn, green and red pepper, jalapeno peppers, mace, turmeric and rice. Mix well.

3. Dust the inside of the pumpkin with the cinnamon. Pack the pumpkin with the filling and replace the pumpkin top. Return pan to oven, add water to cover the bottom of the pan and bake for 45 to 55 minutes.

4. BE CAREFUL. The bottom of the pumpkin may be VERY soft. Wrap the foil from the bottom of the pan up around the pumpkin as you pick it up, this will keep the bottom intact.

When serving, scrape the inside of the pumpkin with the serving spoon and mix the pumpkin into the stuffing.

If you have leftovers do not leave it in the pumpkin. Remove the filling and scrape out the pumpkin and store in your refrigerator or freeze for future use.

KALE CASSEROLE

- ¾ cup brown rice, **COOKED**
- ½ cup cheddar cheese
- 1 lb fresh kale, chopped
- 2 eggs, beaten
- 1 piece of whole grain bread, ground into crumbs.

Combine the cooked rice and cheese. Stir in the beaten eggs. Stir in the chopped kale. Pour into a casserole dish. Top with bread crumbs. Bake at 350 degrees for 35 minutes.

VEGGIE RICE and GARBANZOS with COCONUT

- 2 cups **COOKED** brown rice
- 1 cup coconut milk, divided
- ½ TBL coconut oil
- 2 garlic cloves, minced
- ½ teaspoon cumin powder
- 2-4 cups kale, washed and coarsely chopped
- 1 cup cooked garbanzo beans, drained well (rinse and drain well if canned)
- ½ cup cashews, toasted until golden brown
- Dash cayenne pepper

Warm rice in a large saucepan with ½ cup coconut milk and a small amount of water. Use low heat.

While rice warms, place coconut oil in a large pan on medium high heat. Add garlic and cumin, cook for a brief moment. Add kale and cover until wilted (a couple of minutes usually). Remove lid and add remaining ingredients. Cook until heated through, stirring occasionally.

VARIATIONS: Substitute quinoa or Israeli couscous or Italian couscous for the rice. Substitute chard or collards for the kale. As always, be creative!

VEGGIE PATTIES

- ½ TBL coconut oil
- ¾ cup fresh corn kernels or frozen organic (thawed)
- ½ red bell pepper, finely chopped
- 1 clove garlic, finely chopped
- 1 teaspoon cumin
- Dash cayenne pepper
- ½ cup chopped fresh kale or other leafy green
- 1 carrot, unpeeled and grated
- 1 small sweet potato, grated
- 1 "flax egg" (grind 1/3 cup flax seeds in a blender and add 1 cup water or pure juice)
- ½ cup fresh bread crumbs (try gluten free bread)

In a large skillet heat 1 tablespoon coconut oil over medium high heat. Stir in corn and bell pepper. Cook for 3-4 minutes. Add garlic, cumin and cayenne and cook for 30 seconds. Remove from heat and stir in kale. Add carrot and potato and stir to combine. Add "flax egg."

Stir in enough bread crumbs so that the mixture holds together. Shape mixture into disks and place on a plate. Chill for 1 hour.

Lightly oil a cast iron skillet and cook veggie patties until golden on each side. Freeze unused portions for quick future meals.

VEGETABLE BROWN RICE

- 1 TBL coconut oil
- 1 stalk bok choy, diced
- 2 unpeeled carrots, diced
- 1 garlic cloves, diced
- 3 cups kale or collard greens, chopped
- 1 cup **COOKED** brown rice
- 1 teaspoon paprika
- 1 TBL peanuts (for those birds who need an incentive!)

In a large skillet saute bok choy, carrots and garlic in coconut oil until vegetables are tender. Add kale or collards and continue to saute until greens are wilted (2-3 minutes). Add cooked brown rice to the mixture. Stir in paprika and peanuts.

Vegetables, 57

PARKER'S PERFECT POTPOURRI
by Patricia Sund, http://parrotnation.wordpress.com/

This is a combo-platter using all kinds of things but essentially it utilizes frozen vegetables. Ahem...

Get bags of frozen vegetables without sauce. The aim is to combine as many vegetables using different veggie combos as possible. For instance there are "designer" combos called "Japanese Blend," "Baby Broccoli Mix" or "Italian Blend". Just pay attention to combining the widest variety of veggies as you can: carrots, broccoli, corn, cauliflower, green pepper, peas, yellow squash, zucchini, green beans, snow peas, etc. Always buy a plain bag of chopped kale to add. It's really good for them! Combine the different mixes together in a big Ziploc.

The recipe: Take out the mixed bag and defrost what you intend to use. Microwave it, or let it sit. Grind it up in a food processor and put it in a Tupperware container with a lid.

Now comes the creative part: Add whatever you like that will make things healthy for your birds. I start with adding some healthy seed: Hemp, rape and flax seed go in first.

I grind up fresh sweet potatoes and carrots in a food processor and add that. I'll add any other fresh veggies I have laying around and grind those up as well. I will cook up a batch of brown rice and have this frozen in a baggie in the freezer. Add some of that. They like white rice better. Tough luck; they get brown if I have it! If I have leftover pasta that goes in, slightly cut up if it's big, and if it's elbow or shell pasta it goes in as is. Sometimes I'll add some nuts. Use your imagination!

Cover it and shake the dickens out of it! Open serve and watch them enjoy it...you hope. When I serve it to my birds, it gets a drizzle of flax seed oil.

The best part of this is you can change it up. You're only limited to your imagination. This will keep for 2 days in the fridge. But you get four or five meals out of it, and it's a cinch to make. You get less "tossing overboard" because it's ground. It smells great and it's colorful.

Alternatives and/or additions:
ground up hot peppers, dried pepper flakes, seaweed, cooked quinoa, sesame seeds, sprouts, cooked baby food puree.

VEGETABLE COUSCOUS

½ teaspoon ground turmeric
½ teaspoon ground cinnamon
1 teaspoon ground ginger
A few sprigs of parsley and cilantro, chopped
1 tomato, chopped
7 cups water or unsalted vegetable stock
1 turnip, unpeeled and cut in cubes
½ lb. unpeeled carrots, cut in sticks
¾ lb. butternut squash, peeled, seeded, and cut in chunks
1 zucchini, cut in sticks
1 cup raisins
1 14-oz. can chickpeas, rinsed and drained
2 cups couscous
½ cup slivered almonds

In a pan over medium heat, combine turmeric, cinnamon, ginger, parsley, cilantro, tomato, stock and water. Bring to a boil, reduce heat to low and cook 10 minutes.

Add turnip, carrots and squash. Bring to a boil, and cook 10 minutes. Add zucchini, raisins, and chickpeas. Cook 10 minutes more, or until vegetables are tender.

Cook couscous according to package directions. Serve a bit of vegetables and couscous together. Sprinkle with toasted almonds. Store couscous and vegetables separately for best results.

THYME CARROTS

- Carrots
- Olive oil
- Fresh thyme

Wash organic carrots, but no need to peel. Cut the tips to remove any root fibers. Cut into pieces that are the right size for your parrot. Toss in a bowl with a small amount of olive oil. Scatter the thyme branches over the carrots, and crush a few leaves in the process. Place on baking sheet at 450 degrees for 15-25 minutes, depending on the size.

Several vegetables can be baked in the oven with a touch of oil and spices, in addition to carrots. Try potatoes, eggplant or squashes. Drizzle a bit of olive or coconut oil and sprinkle with rosemary or thyme. Bake at 450.

Vegetables, 59

BIRDIE BAKED TATERS
by Colleen Soehnlein

- Baseball sized potatoes (I do 6 at a time)
- About ½ cup of finely chopped fresh broccoli
- About a half cup of shredded cheddar cheese
- 3 TBLs rice or almond milk
- Two slices cheddar cheese
- Sprouts or milk thistle seed as garnish

Bake potatoes. Allow to cool so that you may handle them. When cool cut in half and scoop out the inside with a spoon. Set the "shells" aside. Mash the middles with a fork. Mix in milk. Mix in the broccoli. Spoon the mix back in to the shells. Cut the cheese and lay on top to decorate. Heat them just a bit to melt the cheese and while it's melted sprinkle with sprouts or milk thistle seeds.

[Potatoes hold heat, so make sure they are not too hot before serving!]

These store well overnight in the fridge for use the next day.

(You can substitute sweet potato for regular potatoes)

CARROT PATTIES

- 3 grated carrots. Use large holes of a cheese grater, not a food processor
- ¾ cup finely chopped celery (2 stalks)
- ¼ cup bread crumbs, make your own with healthy breads
- 2 large eggs, beaten
- ½ cup fresh parsley, finely chopped
- Small amount of coconut oil for cooking

Combine carrots, celery, bread crumbs, eggs, and parsley in a medium bowl. Press the mixture between hands to form the patties.

Heat a large skillet over medium-low heat with a bit of coconut oil.

Cook patties in 2 or 3 batches, until golden brown, 3-4 minutes per side. Serve with a dollop of yogurt, fresh fruit and some chopped greens for a healthy meal.

PUMPKIN SEED and CARROT PATTIES

- 1 cup raw pumpkin seeds
- ½ cup raw sunflower seeds
- 2 eggs
- ½ cup unbleached flour of any grain
- 1 clove garlic, minced
- 1 large carrot, grated very fine
- *Herbs and spices to taste (e.g. 1 teaspoon curry powder and 1 cup organic raisins)

Coarsely grind pumpkin and sunflower seeds in a small processor. Combine eggs, flour, garlic, carrots, and herbs/spices in a medium bowl. Press the mixture between hands to form the patties.

Bake at 350 degrees in the oven, 15 minutes on each side; or heat a large skillet over medium-low heat with a bit of coconut oil. Cook patties in 2 or 3 batches, until golden brown, 3-4 minutes per side.

CARROT and OATMEAL COOKIES

- 1 cup Bob's Redmill garbanzo bean flour
- 1 teaspoon baking powder
- 1 cup rolled, old-fashioned oats
- ⅔ cup chopped walnuts
- 1 cup shredded carrots
- ½ cup real maple syrup, room temperature
- ½ cup applesauce
- 1 TBL coconut oil
- 1 teaspoon grated fresh ginger

Preheat oven to 375 degrees. Line baking sheets with parchment paper.

Whisk together the flour, baking powder and oats. Add the walnuts and carrots. In a separate smaller bowl, whisk the maple syrup, applesauce, coconut oil and ginger. Add this to the flour mixture and stir until just combined.

Spoon onto baking sheets. Bake 10 - 12 minutes or until golden.

Shredded coconut, dried pineapple, or curry might be delicious variations. Cookies or birdie bread are nice additions to morning meals of chopped fresh fruits and veggies, or use small pieces for some special training time together.

Vegetables, 61

SWEET POTATO and BANANA CRUNCH

- Small sweet potato, cooked
- Banana
- 1 TBL pumpkin seeds
- 1 TBL unhulled sesame seeds
- 1 cup organic cereal without sugars of preservatives (e.g. granola or Peace cereals)
- 1 TBL ground flax seed

Mash sweet potato and banana together in a bowl. Stir in pumpkin seeds, sesame seeds and crushed cereal. Stir together and then form into balls (size appropriate to your parrot). Roll in a bit of flax seed for a final nutritious touch. Or just scoop some into your parrot's dish! If you take a bite, you will surely want more. Make sure you make extra.

SWEET POTATO PUFFS
by Carolyn Swicegood, www.landofvos.com

Bake or boil a large sweet potato until soft. Peel and "mash" with:
- 1 cup chopped nuts (pecans, walnuts, almonds, pine nuts)
- 1 banana
- 1 cup Grape-nuts cereal

Add unsweetened apple juice to make the proper consistency to be moist but hold together. Use a melon baller or roll in your hands to make balls or "puffs". Shake them in a bag of sesame seeds, unsweetened coconut flakes, and a little raw wheat germ. Serve or freeze for later use. You can add your birds' favorite treats to this recipe.

CARROT SPREAD

- Carrots
- Chopped walnuts
- Rice cake

Wash organic carrots, but no need to peel. Slice. Steam until just soft, about 10 minutes. Puree in blender. Stir in some finely chopped walnuts. Some birds enjoy a touch of cinnamon or ginger with their carrots. Spread on a piece of rice cake for a healthy treat.

Be creative and make your own spread using different vegetables. Add some chopped nuts, unsulfured dried fruit or spices to peak your bird's interest. Use veggie spreads on unsalted crackers, a slice of apple, or birdie bread.

SWEET POTATO FALAFEL

- 2 medium sweet potatoes
- 1 ½ teaspoons ground cumin
- 2 cloves of garlic, chopped
- 1 ½ teaspoons coriander
- 2 big handfuls of fresh cilantro, chopped (or other chopped greens)
- Juice of half a lemon
- Cup garbanzo/chickpea flour (grind your own or buy Bob's Redmill)
- Splash of coconut oil to grease the cookie sheet
- Sprinkle of unhulled sesame seeds

Preheat the oven to 425 degrees and roast the sweet potatoes whole until just tender - 45 minutes to 1 hour. Turn off the oven, leave the potatoes to cool, then peel. (Or cut in cubes and cook in water on the stove-top until tender).

Combine the sweet potatoes, cumin, garlic, coriander, fresh cilantro, lemon juice and garbanzo flour into a large bowl. Mash until somewhat smooth. Put in the refrigerator for an hour to firm up, or the freezer for 20-30 minutes. The mixture should be sticky (not wet). Add more flour if necessary.

Reheat the oven to 400 degrees. Use two spoons or your hands to make the mixture into ball-like shapes and place on baking sheets. Sprinkle sesame seeds on top and bake for about 15 minutes, until the bases are golden brown.

SAUTEED VEGGIES and GARBANZOS

Take an assortment of veggies such as squashes, peppers, carrots. Cut into small pieces according to your bird's preference (thinly sliced or strips). Saute in a skillet with some walnut oil or coconut oil, adding each vegetable one at a time. Saute each for a couple of minutes before adding the next. If you want the veggies softer, cover the skillet and turn off the heat. Let sit for 5 minutes or so.

Drain and rinse a 15 oz. can of garbanzo beans. Stir the garbanzos in with the veggies and serve.

Many birds (and people too) will enjoy some garlic thrown into the saute process, maybe some spices like basil or thyme or rosemary. Sprinkle the final dish with fresh grated Parmesan cheese. Serve with some brown rice.

Vegetables, 63

SWEET POTATO CASSEROLE

- 6 sweet potatoes
- 1 can (20 oz) crushed pineapple, with juice
- 2 teaspoons cinnamon
- ½ cup chopped pecans (optional)

Bake sweet potatoes on a cookie sheet at 375 degrees for about an hour, or until done.   When cool enough to handle, scoop at the soft potato. Mash the potatoes with a mixer until smooth.   Add the pineapple, juice and cinnamon. Spoon into a baking dish. Sprinkle with nuts on top. Cover and bake for 40 minutes.   Make sure the casserole is cool before serving to the birds!

GINGER CUMIN CARROTS

- ½ teaspoon cumin seeds
- 2 TBLs coconut oil (or olive oil)
- 1 teaspoon minced fresh ginger
- 1 ½ cup sliced carrots
- 2 TBL water
- 1 teaspoon fresh lemon juice
- 1 teaspoon maple syrup

Toast cumin seeds in a small pan over medium heat.   Shake until the seeds start to pop.   Immediately add oil and ginger. Saute for 1 minute.   Stir in the carrots and turn down to medium low.   Add the water, cover and cook for about 2 minutes.   Stir in the lemon juice and maple syrup.

CURRY COCONUT BUTTERNUT SQUASH

- 1 small butternut squash
- 2 TBL coconut oil
- 1 TBL curry powder
- 1 TBL minced fresh ginger
- 1 clove garlic, minced
- ½ cup coconut milk (optional)
- ¼ cup chopped cilantro

Cut the skin off of the squash. Cut into 1" chunks and steam until soft.

In a small skillet, heat the oil and add the curry and ginger. Simmer about 3 minutes and then add the garlic. Simmer a couple of minutes more. Blend the steamed squash and spices together in a blender. In a bowl, combine the squash, coconut milk and cilantro.

BAKED and STUFFED ACORN SQUASH

Steam or bake squash until soft. Cool.

Gently scoop out the squash, protecting the shell. Mash the squash with chopped fruits such as apples, apricots, raisins or unsulfured dried fruits, nuts, cinnamon and other bird healthy favorites. Spoon the mixture back into the squash shell and place in feeding dish.

GREENS and CRANBERRIES

Chop up some greens -- collard, kale, or mustard. Melt some coconut oil in a skillet. Add the greens and some dried cranberries. Stir for 2-3 minutes. Greens will cook very quickly and should not be overcooked. Serve with some steamed sweet potatoes, a dollop of yogurt and soaked grains for a varied, healthy meal.

PINEAPPLE GREENS with PEANUT BUTTER

Bring crushed pineapple and its juice to a simmer. Stir in chopped greens and simmer for 5 more minutes. Mix in a bit of organic peanut butter and fresh cilantro and simmer for 5 more minutes. This would be a good accompaniment to couscous.

LEAFY GREENS can be added to almost every recipe or mixed in with raw fruit or veggies, cooked in omelets, or just hand a leaf to your parrot like it's the most special treat in the world. Use every opportunity possible to include greens in your parrot's diet. Small birds might enjoy a large leaf clipped to the side of the cage. Others have fun with big, dripping wet leaves put on top of the cage. Try wrapping a treat inside a leafy green, like nuts or fruit pieces, and then put this in a foraging toy.

Leafy greens used to be one of the greatest sources of the essential Omega-3; however, non-organic greens have been depleted of many nutrients. Please buy organic when you can, or start your own small garden!

> There are many important ingredients to your parrot's diet, but there can never be enough leafy greens!

Vegetables, 65

CHOP CHOP!
by Patricia Sund, http://parrotnation.wordpress.com/

While I thought people would be interested in the idea of making "Chop" for their birds, I didn't quite anticipate the overwhelming positive response to it. Man! But I think it's terrific and I can just see birds all over the world looking better, feeling spunkier and getting healthier due to their diet of "Chop" along with sprouts, nuts, treats and a formulated pelleted diet. I can also almost feel them getting more active and driving their families a little nuts due to it! But it sure beats having a bird with vitamin deficiencies and liver issues due to an all-seed diet.

Christina Giordano of Angels of Flight decided to take my suggestion of throwing a "Chop Party." Her birds like Chop so much, she decided to get together with her bird friends and make a huge batch to share with them. When sending out invitations and announcements via e-mail and Facebook, she referred to it as "...kinda like a Mary Kay Party, only with vegetables." I thought this was hilarious!

Before the party she e-mailed me the list of ingredients that were being utilized into the chop, and it was extensive. This is what she used:

Broccoli florets, sweet peas, sweet corn, butternut squash, yams / sweet potato, collard greens, zucchini, tri-colored pepper mix, jalapenos peppers, kale, mustard greens, cauliflower florets, asparagus, carrots, celery, romaine lettuce, spinach, yellow squash, parsley, cilantro, ginger root, dandelion greens, escarole, endive, arugula, bell pepper, chard, bib lettuce, bok choy, watercress, cranberries, basil, oregano, dill, banana pepper, radish, broccoli slaw, snap peas, cabbage, red cabbage, parsnips, turnip greens, okra, rosemary, thyme, nori – Japanese seaweed, unsweetened coconut, grains, seed and pasta, muesli, celery seed, hemp seed, wheat germ, brown flax seed, red quinoa, wild / brown rice, spelt, whole grain pasta spirals, and Higgins leafy greens & herbs.

It's a very well-rounded list of ingredients and seems like quite a balanced selection of items. There is enough seed to keep them interested, yet it's loaded with "good for them" green and orange vegetables.

When the party started, they divided up the work into stations. This is a shot of some purple cabbage being added to other chopped vegetables:

Once they got the vegetables chopped, they were challenged with finding a container big enough to hold it all in order to mix it. Christina had never made such a huge batch before, and as we were discussing it over the phone, it hit me. I told her to simply clean and disinfect the bathtub and use that to mix it. Then load the mixed chop back into the five gallon buckets, take it to the kitchen and begin packaging it there. This is what it looked like before Christina got her hands on it.

It worked beautifully. And there was a never-thought-of-before bonus; as she was mixing it, the excess moisture from the Chop filtered out and down the tub drain. Bingo! It was perfect!

At the end of the day, they had 1800 meals. While this was going on, I was on the phone with them sporadically, asking how it was going. As they were working, they were posting the photos and video on Facebook so everyone could see the progress. People were posting questions and I was fielding the questions and doing a "play-by-play" if you will, on Facebook while they were assembling the Chop and putting up the shots and the video. (http://parrotnation.wordpress.com/tag/chop-recipe/)

It was a ton of fun for everyone and the Chop they made was gorgeous. Here they are packing the "Chop." Yes, I am fully aware of what it "looks" like they packing, but I assure you it is "Chop!"

This recipe is for large volumes! Use fewer proportions for a lesser volume.

Vegetables, 67

FRUIT SECTION

- Fruit Section, General Info — Page 69
- Banana Blueberry Pumpkin Waffles/Pancakes — Page 70
- More Fruit Pancakes — Page 70
- Curry Couscous — Page 71
- Mango Salsa — Page 71
- Iced Fruit Juice — Page 71
- Apricot Couscous — Page 72
- Apricot Carrots — Page 72
- Apple, Beet and Orange Salad — Page 73
- Apples, Cranberries And Couscous — Page 73
- Birdie Muffins — Page 74
- Banana Macadamia Bread — Page 74
- Banana Bread — Page 75
- Banana Zucchini Bread — Page 75
- Baked Apples, Cinnamon And Walnuts — Page 76
- Fruit And Sprout Salsa — Page 76
- Fruit Rice Cakes — Page 76
- Coconut And Fruit Ambrosia — Page 76
- Cherries, Gout And Uric Acid — Page 77
- Carrot And Cherry Salad — Page 77
- Apple Coleslaw — Page 78
- Polenta With Dried Fruit Compote — Page 78
- Cowboy Nutriberries — Page 79
- Cantaloupe Seed Delight — Page 79
- Jicama And Basil Fruit Salad — Page 80
- Pomegranates — Page 80
- Cantaloupe and Cucumber Salad — Page 80
- Sunday Morning Raw Fruity Oats — Page 81
- Banana Nut Brittle — Page 81

As with vegetables, larger birds may enjoy large chunks to hold; and if the produce is organic, they can do their own peeling. Smaller birds will do better with smaller pieces, and if they are overly picky, make a puree. The key to good nutrition is variety! **It's not just what you provide, it is what they eat.**

FRUIT SECTION

As with vegetables, the deeply colored tropical fruits usually contain more nutrition. Tropical fruits are often the type which wild parrots eat in their native habitats as well. Make sure they do not swallow pits or apple seeds as these can be toxic. Get to know your bird, most birds naturally know not to eat the pits.

Some species, like Eclectus and cockatoos, need a higher proportion of fruit in their diets.

Nutritional fruits include:
* Mango
* Kiwi
* Berries
* Pomegranates
* Pineapple
* Cranberries
* Papaya (including the peppery seeds)
* Cantaloupe and other melons, including the seeds
* Peaches
* Nectarines
* Apricots
* Apples - pectin helps fight zinc toxicity
* Bananas
* Oranges. Also can squeeze orange juice to help prevent food spoilage, or to neutralize oxalic acid which binds calcium and can be found in spinach and chard
* Cherries, helps fight uric acid
* Pears
* Grapes
* Grapefruit
* Tangerines

When using dried fruits, always make sure these are unsulfured. Sulfur dioxide is a very potent preservative and is not recommended for parrots!

Dehydrators are useful for preserving fruits or making special treats.

BANANA BLUEBERRY PUMPKIN WAFFLES (or Pancakes)
by Colleen Soehnlein

- 2 cups flour, recommend ground whole oats
- 3 teaspoon baking powder
- 1 ½ cups blueberry juice
- 1 cup mashed ripe banana
- ½ cup pumpkin puree
- ½ cup fresh or dried blueberries
- ½ cup finely chopped nuts – your choice
- 3 eggs

Preheat waffle iron or skillet/griddle for pancakes. In a large bowl, combine the flour, baking powder, and fruit. In a medium bowl beat the eggs until foamy. Add banana, pumpkin, and juice. Add the wet mixture to the dry ingredients in the large bowl and mix just until moistened.

Cook on waffle iron according to your manufacturer's direction or cook as pancakes – either way the birds will be thrilled!!

Serve warm or cool on rack before freezing.

MORE FRUIT PANCAKES

- 1 cup flour (unbleached). Good choices: ground oatmeal, garbanzo
- ⅓ cup sesame seed meal
- 1 TBL baking powder
- ¾ cup raw brown rice. Cook according to directions.
- 3 eggs, separated
- 1 ½ cup milk (rice, oat, almond, soy)
- ¼ cup applesauce
- 1 cup fresh fruit (apples, pears, peaches, bananas, berries)

Stir together the flour, sesame seed meal, and baking powder. Beat the eggs yolks, blend in the milk and applesauce, then stir in the rice. Blend well so there are no lumps of grain. Stir the wet ingredients into the dry, using the fewest strokes possible, just be sure the dry ingredients are wet. Fold in the egg whites that have been beaten until stiff. Gently fold in the fruit. Bake on a hot, oiled griddle.

CURRY COUSCOUS
by Leigh Ann Hartsfield

- 2 cups filtered water or low sodium vegetable broth
- 2 teaspoon curry powder
- 1 TBL extra-virgin olive oil
- A handful of unsulfured dark or golden raisins
- 1 cup whole wheat couscous
- 1 carrot, shredded or grated
- 1 navel orange, peeled and chopped
- ¼ cup thinly sliced almonds

Bring water or broth to a boil with curry powder and raisins. Place couscous in a heat proof bowl. Add boiling liquid, cover, and let stand for 10 minutes. Fluff with a fork and add carrot, orange bits, and almonds.

This recipe makes a very nice meal when topped with mango salsa (next recipe).

MANGO SALSA
by Leigh Ann Hartsfield

1 ripe mango, peeled and diced
1 red bell pepper, diced
1 Serrano pepper, seeded and finely chopped
1 inch fresh ginger root, peeled and grated
¼ English cucumber, peeled and chopped
¼ cup fresh cilantro, chopped
Juice of 1 lime

Combine all ingredients in a small bowl. Tastes blend very nicely after a couple of hours in the refrigerator. This recipe makes about 4 small meals for medium sized parrots. Double or triple the recipe if you want to freeze in meal sized portions for later use. This salsa also makes an excellent topping for curry couscous.

ICED FRUIT JUICE

- Favorite fruits, pureed in a blender; or
- Pure fruit juice (no sugar or preservatives!!)

Pour into an ice cube tray and freeze. Great for those hot summer days.

APRICOT COUSCOUS

- 2 TBL coconut oil
- 2 medium garlic cloves, minced
- ¼ teaspoon ground cinnamon
- ⅛ teaspoon ground ginger
- ⅛ teaspoon turmeric
- 1 cup plain couscous
- 1 ⅓ cups homemade chicken broth or mango juice
- ¼ cup finely chopped unsulfured dried apricots
- 3 TBL dried raisins
- ¼ cup shelled pistachio nuts (no salt!), chopped
- 2 TBL minced fresh parsley leaves

Heat oil over medium heat in a medium saucepan. Add garlic, cinnamon, ginger, and turmeric. Saute for a minute or so. Add couscous. Stir until well coated with spices and oil, 1 to 2 minutes. Add chicken broth or juice, apricots and raisins. Bring to a low boil, remove from heat, cover and let stand until couscous has absorbed all the liquid, about 5 minutes. Fluff couscous with a fork, then stir in pistachios and parsley.

French or Moroccan couscous is a small grain and cooks very quickly. It is an easy fix for busy days. Stir in some fruit, greens and a few veggies for a complete meal.

Israeli couscous is pellet size and takes about 15 minutes. It also can be combined with other foods for a simple, fast and scrumptious meal.

APRICOT CARROTS

- 2 TBL coconut oil
- 6 carrots, unpeeled and sliced into thin rounds
- ½ cup fresh, unsalted chicken broth or juice
- ½ cup unsulfured dried apricots, coarsely chopped
- 1 teaspoon honey
- 1 teaspoon balsamic vinegar
- ¼ teaspoon ground cinnamon

In a medium saucepan, saute the carrots in the oil over medium heat for 3 minutes. Add chicken broth or water, apricots, honey, balsamic vinegar, and cinnamon to the carrots. Cover and simmer 4 minutes.

APPLE, BEET and ORANGE SALAD

- 2 fresh beets with greens
- 1 orange
- 2 unpeeled granny smith apples, thinly sliced
- 1 TBL flax oil
- 1 TBL apple cider vinegar
- 1 clove garlic, minced
- 2 TBL unsalted sunflower seeds

Scrub beets with a brush and place in a small saucepan. Add water to cover and bring to a boil. Cover, reduce heat and simmer 20 minutes or until tender. Drain and let cool. Cut each beet into the size appropriate for your bird.

Peel and section orange, cut into chunks Chop apples and beets, add to orange. Shred the raw beet greens and add.

Combine oil, vinegar and garlic in a jar. Shake and pour over beets and fruit mixture. Toss everything gently and spoon into bird bowls. Sprinkle with sunflower seeds.

APPLES, CRANBERRIES and COUSCOUS

- 2 TBLs coconut oil
- 2 cups Israeli couscous
- 4 cups water or fresh chicken broth (no salt)
- ¼ cup chopped parsley
- 1 ½ tablespoons chopped fresh rosemary leaves
- 1 teaspoon chopped fresh thyme leaves
- 1 medium green apple, diced
- 1 cup dried cranberries
- ½ cup slivered almonds

In a medium saucepan, heat the coconut oil on medium-high heat. Add the couscous. Stir occasionally until slightly browned and aromatic, about 3 to 5 minutes. Add the water or broth and bring to a boil. Simmer 10 to 12 minutes or until the liquid has evaporated.

Let the couscous cool. Add the parsley, rosemary, thyme, apple and cranberries. Gently blend.   Top with almonds when serving.

Fruits, 73

BIRDIE MUFFINS
by Colleen Soehnlein

This is my favorite and my stand-by. There are always a few muffins in my freezer – good in a pinch. And the birds here love them. I hope you'll try it for your flock....

- 2 pounds whole wheat flour
- 8 ounces quick cooking steal cut oats
- 8 ounces walnut pieces
- 8 ounces dried mixed berries
- 2 TBL baking powder (optional)
- 3 very ripe bananas
- 4 eggs
- 4 cups organic wild blueberry juice

Mix dry ingredients together in a large bowl. Set aside.

Mash bananas. Mix in eggs. Add the blueberry juice.

Add wet ingredients to dry. Don't over mix!! Fill large muffin tins or mini loaf pans to heaping. Bake for 35 minutes at 350 degrees. Remove them from the oven. Cool on a wire rack and wrap in aluminum foil for freezing.

BANANA MACADAMIA BREAD

- 2 cups ground oats to make flour
- 1-½ teaspoons ground cinnamon
- 1-¼ cups mashed ripe bananas
- ⅓ cup pure juice
- 1 teaspoon apple cider vinegar
- ¼ cup applesauce (no sugar)
- 1 egg
- 1 cup macadamia nuts, chopped

Preheat oven to 350 degrees F. Lightly oil a 10" cast iron skillet.

In a large bowl, combine flour, cinnamon, bananas, juice, vinegar, applesauce and egg. Beat at medium speed of electric mixer for 30 seconds or until dry ingredients are just moistened. Stir in macadamia nuts. Spoon batter into skillet. Bake at 350 degrees for an hour or until toothpick comes out clean.

BANANA BREAD

- 2 cups ground oats to make flour
- 2 TBL applesauce (no sugar)
- 2 ripe bananas, mashed
- ½ cup chopped walnuts
- ¼ cup water or unsweetened juice

Preheat the oven to 350 degrees. Mix all the ingredients. If the batter is not thick, add small amounts of flour to thicken. Bake in a large cast iron skillet or loaf pan for 50 minutes. Test doneness with a toothpick. Use in 2-3 days, freeze unused portions.

BANANA ZUCCHINI BREAD

- 2 cups ground oats to make flour
- 1 teaspoon ground cinnamon
- ¼ teaspoon ground nutmeg
- 2 large eggs
- ¼ cup applesauce (no sugar)
- ½ cup yogurt
- 1 cup mashed bananas
- 1 cup grated zucchini, excess water squeezed out
- ½ cup chopped brazil nuts or walnuts

Preheat oven to 350 F. Lightly oil a 10" cast iron skillet or large muffin tins.

In a medium bowl, mix together flour, cinnamon, and nutmeg. Set aside.

In a large bowl, whisk eggs and add applesauce and yogurt. Stir in banana. Stir in flour mixture. Fold in zucchini and nuts.

Pour into cast iron skillet or muffin tins. Bake about 45 minutes to 1 hour for the bread or about 25 to 30 minutes for the muffins, until center tests done with a toothpick.

Fruits, 75

BAKED APPLES, CINNAMON and WALNUTS

- 2 cored, green apples
- 1 cup unsweetened pomegranate juice
- 1 teaspoon cinnamon
- ½ cup chopped walnuts

Preheat the oven to 350 degrees. Core the apples (do not peel) and place in a baking dish. Pour the pomegranate juice over the apples. Sprinkle with cinnamon. Bake for 30 minutes. Baste as needed, the juice will make a syrup. Top with chopped walnuts. Cool before serving!

FRUIT and SPROUT SALSA

- ½ mango, cut in sizes appropriate for your parrot
- 1 cup cantaloupe, cut in sizes appropriate for your parrot
- chopped cilantro and/or parsley
- ½ small jalapeno, diced or chopped
- ½ red bell pepper, chopped
- ½ cup fresh sprouts (e.g. mung, lentil)
- Squeeze of orange, pineapple or lime juice

Mix all together and serve. If people wish to share, add some chopped red onions to their portion.

FRUIT RICE CAKES

- Rice cake
- Peanut or almond butter
- Thinly sliced fruit

Put a thin layer of peanut or almond butter on a rice cake. Thinly slice fruit like banana, kiwi, apple and/or strawberries and layer on top. Sprinkle with a bit of cinnamon. Substitute applesauce for the peanut butter for those perch potatoes on a diet.

COCONUT AND FRUIT AMBROSIA

- 1 large ripe mango, chopped
- 1 fresh nectarine, chopped
- 1 fresh apricot, chopped
- Juice of one orange
- Grated coconut to taste

Combine ingredients in a bowl and stir well.

CHERRIES have restorative powers

Cherries can help reduce uric acid, which leads to gout. This is a common problem for seniors or birds that have been on a high protein diet. Organic cherries are preferred as non-organic ones may have high levels of pesticides. Fresh cherry season is from June to August. When cherries are not in season, try pure cherry juice in baked foods or let your bird enjoy a bit of juice from a bowl.

DOES YOUR BIRD HAVE GOUT OR HIGH URIC ACID??

- Gout occurs when crystals of uric acid form in the fluid surrounding a joint. It is a form of arthritis
- Associated with the kidneys' inability to remove nitrogen waste
- Articular gout affects the joints of the lower legs; most common in budgies
- Visceral gout affects the internal organs and is very difficult to diagnose. Cause may be excess protein or improper calcium levels
- Cherries eliminate gout quickly, using fresh, dried or frozen types.
- Black cherry juice concentrate can be added to the drinking water or soak the parrot's favorite dry food in the concentrate.

CARROT and CHERRY SALAD

- 6 cups grated carrots (about 8 carrots)
- ¼ cup apple juice
- 1 cup chopped walnuts
- 1 TBL cumin seeds
- 1 TBL coriander seeds
- 1 cup dried unsulfured cherries
- ¼ cup chopped cilantro or parsley
- Dash of cayenne

Toss carrots with apple juice. Combine walnuts, cumin seeds and coriander seeds in heavy skillet. Toast over medium-high heat 5 minutes, or until beginning to brown, stirring constantly. Add walnut mixture, dried cherries, cilantro and cayenne to carrots.

APPLE COLESLAW

- 2 cups thinly sliced green cabbage
- 1 apple, cored and seeds removed, julienned
- 1 TBL jalapeno
- ¼ cup raisins
- ¼ cup toasted slivered almonds
- 1 TBL chopped mint (optional)

In a medium mixing bowl, combine all of the ingredients. Mix thoroughly.

POLENTA WITH DRIED FRUIT COMPOTE

- 2½ cups pineapple, mango or orange juice
- 1 TBL fresh lemon juice
- ¼ teaspoon cinnamon
- ¼ cup honey
- 10 dried unsulfured apricots, chopped or diced or minced
- 1 cup polenta
- 4 cups water
- ¾ cup coarsely chopped walnuts

Combine the pineapple juice, lemon juice, cinnamon and honey in a medium sized saucepan and stir. Bring to a simmer on high heat and add apricots. Turn the heat to lowest level. Simmer gently for about 5 minutes.

While juice and apricots are simmering, start cooking polenta by bringing 4 cups water to a boil in a medium saucepan. Add polenta to boiling water slowly stirring constantly. Reduce heat to low and cook for about 15 minutes stirring to make sure it doesn't get lumpy. If it starts to get too thick add a little more hot water.

Remove apricots from sauce with a slotted spoon to a shallow bowl and turn the heat to high. Reduce the liquid to about half. Return fruit and add walnuts to sauce and serve over bowl of polenta.

When making polenta, allow time to stir almost constantly so it does not get lumpy. Be sure to cook on low to make sure it does not get too thick before it is fully cooked. The fruit sauce needs to reduce by half to keep the compote thick, however, the birds probably won't care about the consistency!

COWBOY NUTRIBERRIES
(Apologies, author unknown)

- 1 cup of dried unsulfured fruit such as papaya, cherries, cranberries, blueberries, and / or pineapple
- 2 tablespoon of coconut
- ½ cup of old fashioned oatmeal
- ½ cup of raisins or trail mix (no sulfur dioxide, salt or chocolate)
- ¼ cup of seeds and /or crushed nuts
- 2 TBLs of peanut butter
- 1 TBL honey

Blend all the dry ingredients in a food processor until chopped finely. Place mixture into a bowl, add peanut butter and honey. Mix very well until the mixture is sticky. If it seems too dry, add ½ cup of applesauce.

Roll mixture into small ½ inch ball and place on a cookie sheet. Bake at 325 for about 18 minutes. Cool and serve.

CANTALOUPE SEED DELIGHT (Dehydrator)
by Tony Rosa, Jr.

Cantaloupe and honeydew melon pulp and seeds (save in the freezer until you have enough). Thaw and put in the blender with some apple or orange juice.

Add:
- Carrot pulp
- Bee Pollen
- Wheat germ
- Walnuts
- Cashews
- Pecans
- Pinenuts
- Flaxseed oil
- Apples and bananas
- Cinnamon
- Honey

Can add flour to thicken if necessary. Put on a baking sheet and bake at 350 degrees for 50 minutes to an hour. Let cool. Cut into small squares or roll into balls and put into a dehydrator for 1.5 days. Enjoy!

JICAMA AND BASIL FRUIT SALAD

- 1 cup organic grapes (seeded or seedless)
- 1 cup cantaloupe or honeydew, cubed
- 1 cup mango, cubed
- 1 cup pineapple chunks
- 1 cup orange, peeled, sliced and quartered
- 1 cup nectarine, cubed
- ½ cup strawberries, halved
- ½ cup jicama, peeled, cut in slivers or small chunks
- ¼ cup orange juice
- 1 TBL fresh basil, chopped

Combine all ingredients, mix gently.

POMEGRANATES
by Kris Porter (www.parrotenrichment.com)

Make a cut through the crown of the pomegranate, halfway through the fruit. Use your fingers to pry open the fruit the rest of the way. Work over a rimmed baking sheet lined with parchment or wax paper, so that as you open the fruit, any loose seeds fall onto the parchment paper. Make a second cut on each half, again half-way through the fruit, starting at the crown. Again use your fingers to pry open the pomegranate. Working over the baking sheet, use your fingers to pry away the seeds from the peel and membranes. Once you have de-seeded your pomegranate spread them in a single layer on the lined baking sheet. Place in freezer for 2 hours or until frozen. Once frozen, put them into a freezer bag or container and store them in the freezer for up to 6 months.

CANTALOUPE AND CUCUMBER SALAD

- ½ cup yogurt, preferably Greek-style
- Cantaloupe, cut into bite-size pieces
- Cucumber, cut into bite-size pieces
- Celery, thinly sliced
- Chopped fresh mint
- Toasted sliced almonds

Whisk the yogurt. Add the cantaloupe, cucumber, celery and mint. Toss to combine. Sprinkle with toasted almonds. Some birds might prefer their yogurt on the side.

SUNDAY MORNING RAW FRUITY OATS

Fruity, chewy, chunky, and nutty, it begins by putting the grain to soak before bedtime. The next morning breakfast comes together quickly, bursting with goodness.

- ½ cup steel cut Scottish oats
- Water
- 1 large apple, cored and diced (do not peel)
- 1 pear, chopped or any favorite fruit in season
- 2 TBL walnut pieces
- 2 TBL pecan pieces
- 2 TBL unhulled sesame seeds
- 2 TBL flax seed meal
- ⅓ cup dried, unsulfured fruit (berries, papaya, mango...)
- 1 teaspoon ground cinnamon
- 1 ripe banana, mashed

Put oats into a jar or bowl and cover with warm water by one-inch. Soak overnight.

In the morning, strain oats in a fine mesh. Transfer to a medium-size bowl. Add apple, pear, nuts, seeds, dried fruit, and cinnamon and toss to combine ingredients. Fruit can be chunks, grated or minced, depending on the preferences of your parrot.

Top mixture with mashed or chunks of banana. An extra sprinkle of a favored condiment on top gives each serving a special "parrot appeal."

BANANA NUT BRITTLE (Dehydrator)
Cherie Soria, www.RawFoodChef.com

- 2 ½ cups unsulfured dried fruit
- 8 bananas -- peeled
- 3 cups almonds -- roughly chopped
- 3 cups dried, shaved coconut
- ¼ cup flax meal

Blend bananas, dried fruit, and flax meal until smooth. Stir in nuts and coconut. Evenly spread 4 cups of mixture on a dehydrator tray lined with a teflex sheet. Score into the size and shape you want (e.g. 4 x 6 to create 24 rectangles). Dehydrate at 105 degrees for 12 hours, then flip them over and continue dehydrating for another 12 hours or until crispy. Store in a sealed container in the refrigerator or freezer for up to 4 months. Reprinted with permission.

GRAINS

- Types Of Grains   Page 83
- Cooking Grains   Page 84
- Whole Grain Bases   Page 85
- Grains for Sprouting   Page 86
- Franco's Favorite Breakfast   Page 87
- Snowday Breakfast   Page 87
- Birdie Breakfast   Page 88
- Two-Grain Pilaf   Page 88
- Quinoa Parrot Patty-Cakes   Page 89
- Quinoa Pilaf   Page 90
- Quinoa Mash Dinner   Page 91
- Quinoa Cereal And Fresh Fruit   Page 91
- Quinoa Salad   Page 92
- Quinoa And Vegetable Pilaf   Page 92
- Tropical Risotto   Page 93
- Walnut Cheddar Loaf   Page 93
- Kashi Salad   Page 93
- Curry Corn Bread   Page 94
- Oats And Fruit   Page 95
- Cinnamon And Oats   Page 95
- Oat Groats   Page 95
- Cream Of Wheat Dumplings   Page 96
- Parmesan Rice   Page 97
- Sesame Vegetable Rice   Page 97
- Arroz Guisado (Rice Stew)   Page 97
- Elizabeth's Mash Recipe   Page 98-99
- Spicy Quinoa   Page 99
- Old Fashioned Oatmeal   Page 100
- George's Whole Grain Pilaf   Page 100
- Mojito's Bulgar, Quinoa, Parsley & Dill   Page 100
- Brown Rice, Fruit And Nuts   Page 101
- Sesame Rice Parrot-Puffs   Page 101
- Flax Sesame Crackers   Page 101
- Rice, Millet And Lentils   Page 102
- Millet With Dried Fruit Compote   Page 102
- Fruited Millet   Page 102
- Trixie's French Toast   Page 103
- Quinoa Pudding   Page 103

TYPES OF GRAINS

Grains come in a wide variety of textures and tastes, and these can be a very substantial part of a bird's diet. Great grains include barley, quinoa, brown rice, amaranth, wheat berries, kamut, spelt, buckwheat, rye berries, oat groats, millet, teff and couscous. For best nutritional value, soak or sprout these grains. Smaller birds especially love and thrive on soaked grains! Grains can also be cooked. Here are tips about three of these powerhouses - quinoa, brown rice and barley.

QUINOA (pronounced "keen-wah") was considered the "mother grain" by the Inca Indians. Quinoa contains all the amino acids, so it is a complete protein, with an overall protein content of 16-18%. Most other grains do not contain the important amino acid lysine. Quinoa is also gluten free!

Once cooked, it increases to 4X the original volume. Prior to cooking, rinse the grains in cool water to remove the bitter coating called saponin. This coating protects it from being eaten in the field by birds.

BROWN RICE is far more nutritious than white rice because it is less processed. White rice is basically a refined starch with minimal value. Although brown rice takes a bit longer to cook, it's worth it. To save time, make a batch and freeze in portions. It is also rich in selenium, an important mineral for some species like African greys.

BARLEY: **Hulled** barley (has the hull) is very nutritious, and especially high in calcium. The two outer layers are removed, leaving the bran intact. Cooking time is about an hour. Pre-soaking for several hours in advance will further enhance the nutritional value. Cinnamon, garlic and/or thyme are nice spices for barley. **Barley will blossom, so 1 cup raw can equal 3-4 cups cooked.**

Pearled barley is extensively processed, with two outer layers and the bran removed to make it less chewy. This processing also removes most of its inherent nutrition. It cooks in 30-45 minutes.

Other tasty grains include groats, couscous, millet, kamut, whole grain bread or toast, unfortified/unsweetened cereals, wild rice, and old fashioned oatmeal.

COOKING GRAINS

To add more variety, try mixing grains. Here is some information about proportions of water (or juice) to the grain, and cooking time. Be creative, and your bird will learn to expand her likes and dietary options!

Instead of measuring exact proportions of liquid, try cooking in a larger amount of liquid and then drain well once the grain is cooked. For those of us who may let the bottom of the pan scorch, this might be an easier approach! Rice cookers are also an easy way to cook most grains.

ADDING JUICE: To add a boost of flavor and nutrition, grains can be cooked with juice instead of water, or in some portion. However, make SURE the juice is pure, unsweetened, and without supplements or additives. Organic is always recommended. Good juices to use are carrot, mango, pineapple, orange, cherry or tropical blends.

Here is some general information about cooking various grains:

GRAIN	LIQUID PROPORTION	COOKING TIME
Oat Groats (soak first if possible)	3:1	50-60 minutes
Buckwheat Groats	2:1	15-20 minutes
Red Quinoa	2:1	5-7 minutes
White Quinoa	2:1	10-15 minutes
Kamut	3:1	60 minutes
Rye Berries	4:1	90 minutes
Brown Rice	2:1	45-50 minutes
Spelt	3:1	60 minutes
Millet	1.25:0.5	20 minutes
Hulled Barley	4:1	60 minutes
Steel Cut Oats	3:1	30-45 minutes
Amaranth	2:1	20-25 minutes
Wheat berries	3.5:1	50-60 minutes
French Couscous	1.5:1	1 minute, sit for 5 minutes
Israeli Couscous	1.5:1	Saute in oil first, 10-12 minutes

Grains with the highest levels of calcium include: brown rice (2%), oat groats (2%), quinoa (2%), wheat berries (2%), couscous (2%) and amaranth (8%).

Almost all grains include substantial iron: oat groats (10%), rice (4%), quinoa (20%), buckwheat groats (6%), millet (20%), kamut (6%), rye (6%), spelt (15%), wheat berries (10%), couscous (4%) and amaranth (20%).

These percentages are based on 1 cup and the daily value for humans, but give us a sense of the general nutritional content.

WHOLE GRAIN BASES

Whole grains are much more nutrient dense that grains that have been stripped of their hulls and bran. Nutritious whole grains include: brown rice, barley, quinoa, millet, oats, wheat, kamut, amaranth, rye and spelt. Whole grains can be soaked, sprouted or cooked.

Bases can be used as the start of a meal. Supplement with vegetables, legumes and condiments. Adjust amount cooked according to your bird's needs. Cooked grains can be frozen for use later. Be creative - add some chopped veggies and some condiments such as nuts, pumpkin seeds etc for a complete meal. See more about condiments on page 17.

QUINOA FOR A BASE

Rinse quinoa and drain. Combine 2 parts water to 1 part quinoa. Bring to a boil. Lower to simmer and cook for 5-7 minutes. Stir in some chopped greens in the last minute or so.

BROWN RICE FOR A BASE

Bring 1 cup brown rice and 2 cups water to a boil. Lower to simmer, cover and cook for 50 minutes. Brown rice by itself is a perfect base, very nutritious! Cook with carrot juice instead of water for a delightful and yummy addition to any meal.

MILLET FOR A BASE

Rinse 1 cup millet and drain. Bring millet and 2 cups boiling water to a boil. For moister millet, use 3 cups of liquid (recommended).

Reduce the heat and cover. Simmer until all the liquid has been absorbed, 20-25 minutes. Turn off heat and let stand, covered, for 5 minutes. Fluff immediately with a fork. Makes 3 ½ to 4 cups cooked millet. Stores in refrigerator for 3-4 days.

COUSCOUS FOR A BASE

French couscous (small grain) is fast and yummy. Combine 2 parts water to 1 part couscous. Complimentary additions include dried unsulfured fruits, cinnamon or curry. Bring to a boil. Remove from heat and let sit for 5 minutes.

BAKING HULLED BARLEY FOR A BASE

Place 1 cup hulled barley into a one-and-a-half quart glass baking dish. Add 2 ½ cups boiling water to the dish, stirring to combine. Cover the dish tightly. Bake at 375 degrees for 1 hour. Hulled barley preserves the bran, and is much more nutritious than pearled barley.

Grains 85

GRAINS FOR SPROUTING
by Laura Ford
(See directions page 25)

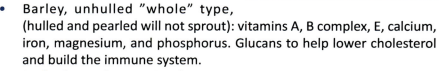

- Amaranth: vitamins A, B, C and E, calcium, iron, magnesium, niacin, phosphorus, potassium, amino acids, protein: 15%.
  Soak 3-5 hours, harvest 2-3 days.
- Barley, unhulled "whole" type, (hulled and pearled will not sprout): vitamins A, B complex, E, calcium, iron, magnesium, and phosphorus. Glucans to help lower cholesterol and build the immune system.
  Soak 6 hours, harvest 2-3 days
- Buckwheat: Raw buckwheat is white, green or light brown, toasted buckwheat is medium brown and will not sprout. Helps flush cholesterol from the body. Vitamins A, B, C and E, calcium, iron, magnesium, niacin, phosphorus, potassium, all amino acids protein: 15%.
  Soak 6 hours, Harvest 3-4 days
- Field Corn: soak 12-18 hours, very slow to germinate Popcorn: vitamins A, B, C and E, calcium, iron, phosphorus, amino acids, protein: 25%. Cleaner than field corn, and very sweet, a favorite of most parrots.
  Soak 12-18 hours, ready to eat after soaking, slow to sprout.
- Kamut: ancient Egyptian wheat. Vitamins B, C and E, calcium, iron, magnesium, pantothenic acid, phosphorus, amino acids, protein: 15%.
  Soak 6-12 hours, ready in 2-3 days.
- Millet, unhulled: vitamin B, E, protein. Soak 8 hours, ready in 2-3 days.
- Oats, unhulled (oat groats will not sprout): vitamins A, B, C and E, calcium, iron, magnesium, niacin, phosphorus, potassium, amino acids, protein: 15%. Good for immune system and skin disorders unless bird is sensitive to gluten. Soak 8 hours, ready in 1-2 days.
- Quinoa: vitamins B1, B2, B3, B6, folacin, copper, iron, magnesium, phosphorus, potassium, zinc and protein. Soak 2-4 hours, harvest 1-2 days.
- Teff: a very tiny, sweet sprout that parrots adore.
  Soak 3-4 hours, harvest 1-2 days
- Triticale (a cross of wheat & rye): vitamins B, C and E, calcium, iron, magnesium, pantothenic acid, phosphorus, amino acids, protein: 15%.
  Soak 6-12 hours, ready in 2-3 days.
- Wheat: B complex, C, E, folacin, iron, magnesium, manganese, calcium, pantothenic acid, phosphorus, omega-6, amino acids, protein: 15%. Flavor is sweetest when tail first appears.
  Soak for 12 hours, harvest in 2-3 days.

FRANCO'S FAVORITE BREAKFAST
by Leigh Ann Hartsfield

- 1 cup brown rice
- 1 cup quinoa
- 2 leaves kale, finely chopped
- 1 sweet potato, grated
- 1 clove garlic, finely grated
- 1 cup frozen green peas
- 3 teaspoon turmeric
- Dash of celery leaf from the spice aisle
- Fresh sprouts
- Udo's or other omega oil

Prepare rice and quinoa in separate pans according to package directions. Add kale, sweet potato, garlic, green peas, turmeric, and celery leaf to the brown rice during the last five minutes of cooking time.

Combine rice-veggie-spice mixture with the cooked quinoa. Refrigerate or freeze in meal-sized portions.

Just before serving, combine the rice/quinoa mixture in a 1:1 ratio with fresh sprouts. Add a squirt of omega oil and/or red palm oil.

SNOWDAY BREAKFAST
by Laura Ford

- ½ cup oatmeal
- ½ cup quinoa
- 2 cup water
- ½ cup juice such as apple, orange, peach, mango, etc. (no sugar!)
- Generous teaspoon cinnamon
- ¼ cup unsulfured dried fruits, such as cranberries, cherries, apricots, etc.
- ¼ cup chopped nuts, such as walnuts, almonds, pecans, etc.

Cook approximately 15 minutes, adding additional water if necessary. Serve topped with a spoonful of yogurt.

BIRDIE BREAKFAST
Gudrun Maybaum, www.totallyorganics.com

The following is the recipe my birds get several times a week.
I love quinoa, because it is so very nutritious.

- 1 cup of quinoa
- 2 cups of water
- 2 large carrots
- ½ fennel bulb or 2 stalks of celery or 3-4 brussel sprouts or any other vegetable. I sometimes add some apple cubes.

Bring the water and quinoa to a boil, turn down heat and let it slowly cook until all the water is gone (about 10 minutes).

Put carrots and other vegetables in food processor and puree.

I sometimes add ½ teaspoon of cinnamon or herbs from my garden, like sweet basil, mints, lovage, parsley, thyme, sage or rosemary.

Add the vegetables to quinoa, stir until all is well mixed. Ready to feed!

TWO-GRAIN PILAF

- 2 TBL coconut oil
- ½ cup uncooked buckwheat groats
- ½ cup uncooked quinoa, rinsed
- 2 cups carrots, cut to parrot's preference (and/or sweet potatoes)
- 1 cup vegetable stock (no salt)
- ¾ cup diced dried unsulfured apricots
- 2 cups leafy greens, chopped or cut in slivers

Heat oil in large skillet over medium heat. Sauté groats over medium-high heat about 7 minutes, or until golden. Add quinoa and sauté 2 more minutes. Add carrots, vegetable stock (or water or pure juice, or broth from freshly cooked chicken). Quickly bring to a boil, and then reduce heat to low.

Cook 10-15 minutes, stirring occasionally
and checking for liquid. Add more liquid if too dry. Better to have too much liquid than not enough! Stir in apricots and leafy greens. Cover and let sit for a couple minutes.

QUINOA PARROT PATTY-CAKES

- 1 cup quinoa
- 2 cups water
- 2 medium sweet potatoes, scrubbed and cut into bite-size pieces. If organic, leave the skin on!
- 2 medium carrots, diced (and unpeeled if organic)
- 1 red or yellow bell pepper, diced (seeds are fine)
- ½ cup almond meal
- ½ cup unprocessed flour (ground oatmeal or garbanzo bean or millet flours are great healthy choices).
- ¼ cup water
- ½ teaspoon celery seed
- ½ teaspoon turmeric
- ¼ teaspoon ginger
- ¼ teaspoon cayenne

Preheat the oven to 375 degrees and line 2 baking sheets with parchment paper.

Place the quinoa in a fine mesh strainer. Rinse to remove the natural saponin coating that may leave a slightly bitter taste. Transfer to a 2-quart saucepan and add 2 cups water. Cover and bring to a boil over high heat. Turn the heat down to low and steam for 20 minutes. Remove from the heat and allow to stand, covered, for 10 minutes.

While the quinoa is cooking, place the potato chunks in a saucepan and cover with water. [My preference is to steam in a covered double pan]. Cook over medium high heat for 6 to 8 minutes or until fork tender. Drain and put the potatoes in a large mixing bowl and mash thoroughly.

While the quinoa and potatoes are cooking, cut the carrots and pepper. Add these to the bowl with the mashed potatoes.

Add the almond meal, flour, ¼ cup water, celery seed, turmeric, ginger, cayenne and mix well. When the quinoa is ready, stir it into the patty mixture and mix well to thoroughly incorporate.

Form the mixture into ½-inch thick patties and place on the baking sheets. Bake for 12 minutes. Turn the patties over with a spatula and bake for 10 minutes longer. Remove the patties from the oven and allow to cool before removing from the baking sheet. Freeze unused portions in batches.

Grains, 89

QUINOA PILAF
by Pamela Clark, CVT

- 1 cup quinoa (or other combination of grains)
- 2 cups water
- grated carrots or yams
- whole corn kernels (cut from cob or frozen)
- grated zucchini or broccoli
- ½ cup flax seeds or other
- ½ cup ground walnuts or other
- ½ cup currants (optional)
- 1 teaspoon Udo's Oil blend or African palm oil

Directions for stove-top:
Bring water to a boil and add quinoa. After mixture has come to a boil again, cover and turn heat to medium-low. Cook for five minutes, then add carrots or yams. Cover again and cook for another 10 minutes or until liquid is absorbed. Turn into a bowl and mix with other ingredients. Feel free to experiment with this recipe. You can use almost any combination of fruits and vegetables. (Hint: the quinoa and shredded yams can be cooked together in a rice cooker also.)

Directions for the rice cooker:
Place the desired amount of quinoa into the rice cooker. Add water to the corresponding line. (For example, if I add 5 scoops of quinoa, I will add water to the #5 line.) Place shredded yams or carrots on top. Cover and turn on to cook. The rice cooker will turn off automatically when done.

Turn the cooked quinoa into a large bowl and then add whatever additions you have on hand. Suggestions include:

- Fresh corn cut off the cob (or frozen)
- Roasted or steamed vegetables (or fresh shredded vegetables)
- Frozen peas
- Canned garbanzo beans or soy beans
- Flax seeds
- Sesame seeds
- Raw pumpkin seeds
- Ground or chopped nuts of any type
- Grated cheddar or Parmesan cheese
- Use your imagination

QUINOA MASH DINNER
by Laura Ford

Wash and rinse ½ cup of quinoa, with ½ cup other grain, such as rice, kamut, wheat, buckwheat, etc. Soak for 2-12 hours.

Scrub and finely chop a large sweet potato, place in sauce pan with grains and 2 cups of water, add a generous teaspoon each of cinnamon and cayenne pepper, bring mixture to a boil, then turn down to a simmer for approximately 20 minutes, adding additional water if needed.

While this mixture is cooking, finely chop a good handful of greens such as kale, collards, mustard, turnip, dandelion, etc; as well as about a cup of other seasonal veggies, broccoli, corn, carrots, zucchini, green beans, etc. Add chopped veggies, and greens to sweet potato & grain mixture, cook for about 5 more minutes. Turn off heat.

Add a handful of seasonal (or frozen) berries, or other fruit. Place desired portion into each bird's bowl, squirt in a few drops of an Omega-3 oil.

A spoonful of fresh sprouts, soaked grains, or chopped nuts may also be mixed in at this point. Leftover cooked mixture may be divided and refrigerated or frozen for later serving. Pumpkin or winter squash may be substituted for sweet potato.

QUINOA CEREAL AND FRESH FRUIT

Quinoa
- 1 cup quinoa
- 2 cups water

Topping
- ¼ cup rolled oats
- A combination of favorite fruits, pumpkin seeds and nuts, like:
- ¼ cup blueberries
- 1 TBL pumpkin seeds
- 1 TBL sliced almonds

Rinse the quinoa and combine with water in a saucepan, cover and bring to a boil. Reduce to low, keep covered and simmer for 15 minutes.

Combine ¼ of the quinoa with rolled oats. Top with blueberries, pumpkin seeds and almonds. If humans are sharing, serve with a bit of milk and honey. Save the remaining quinoa for additional servings. Make extra quinoa and store in refrigerator. Add the toppings just before serving.

Called a supergrain, quinoa is highly nutritious and can provide us with all of the body's requirements: protein, carbohydrates, fats, vitamins, minerals and fiber. It is a complete protein, unlike any other grain. Quinoa is gluten free and considered an ideal food for those susceptible to food allergies. Common allergens include grains from the grass family like corn and wheat. Quinoa is a leafy grain, and not in the grass family, so it is a perfect substitute for those that cannot tolerate other grains like wheat, corn, rye, barley, and oats. It is possible that some parrots may also have food allergies.

QUINOA SALAD

- 2 cups quinoa, cooked
- 1 cup carrots, diced
- 1 cup sunflower seeds

Mix all ingredients. For birds just learning to eat grains or whole foods, the sunflower seeds provide a nice incentive to begin "pecking" through nutritious foods. You can add other vegetables or fruits in the future, and reduce the sunflower seeds gradually. If you are sharing this meal with your bird, add garlic, tomatoes, olives, salt and/or vinaigrette dressing.

QUINOA and VEGETABLE PILAF

- 1 cup quinoa
- 1 TBL coconut oil
- ½ cup carrot, diced
- ¼ cup celery, diced
- ½ cup chopped greens like kale
- ½ cup peppers (red, green, orange, and/or yellow), diced
- ½ cup almonds, sliced
- ½ teaspoon oregano
- 2 cloves garlic, crushed

Bring 1 cup quinoa in 2 cups of water to a boil. Reduce to simmer, cover and cook for about 15 minutes.

Meanwhile, saute carrots, celery and peppers in coconut oil for a few minutes until clear but crisp. Stir in oregano and almonds. If you're sharing this dinner, you can dry-roast the almonds first in a skillet until lightly golden.

This recipe can be varied with different vegetables. Be creative!

92, Grains

TROPICAL RISOTTO

- 1 cup Arborio rice
- 2 cups water or pure fruit juice
- 1 15-oz can coconut milk
- 8-oz can organic pineapple (SAVE juice)
- ¼ cup sliced almonds
- ¼ cup raisins and/or dried cranberries or blueberries
- 1 cup banana cut into pieces sized for your bird

Bring water (or juice) with rice to a boil in medium-sized saucepan. When it boils, turn heat to medium low and simmer uncovered, stirring frequently for creaminess. While rice is cooking, prepare the rest of the ingredients.

As water is absorbed in rice, add pineapple juice and keep cooking. When that is absorbed, add the can of coconut milk. As the coconut milk is absorbed, but while still creamy, add the remaining ingredients. Heat for another 2-3 minutes or until the rice is tender. This texture should be juicy and creamy without being runny.

Top with fruits and nuts just before serving, warm or cool. Keep for a day or 2 in the refrigerator or store serving portions in the freezer.

WALNUT CHEDDAR LOAF

- 1 cup ground walnuts
- ½ cup grated cheese
- 1 cup brown rice, cooked
- 2 eggs, beaten

Combine all ingredients. Place in an oiled loaf pan. Bake at 350 degrees for 30 minutes. For larger birds, you can leave the walnuts a bit chunkier.

KASHI SALAD

- 1 package Kashi pilaf mix, prepared according to directions.
- 1 15-ounce can garbanzos, adzuki beans or lentils, drained and rinsed
- 1 15-ounce package organic mixed vegetables, warmed

Stir together. Mix in some fruit and nuts of choice, and sprinkle with condiments.

Grains, 93

CURRY CORNBREAD
by Kris Porter (parrotenrichment.com)

DRY INGREDIENTS
- 3 cups stone ground cornmeal
- 3 cups whole grain flour (for variety try a mix of different flours such as barley, oat, garbanzo, spelt or almond)
- 1 ½ cup rolled oats
- 1 ½ cup 7 grain cereal (this is usually in the bulk food section and made from coarsely ground whole grain hard red wheat, rye, oats, triticale, barley, brown rice, oat bran and flaxseed)
- ⅓ cup pumpkin seed
- ⅓ cup sunflower seed
- ¾ cup millet
- 1 TBL curry powder

Mix above dry ingredients together in very large bowl

VEGETABLES

- About 3 cups finely chopped vegetables: broccoli; beets; chayote squash; zucchini squash; mustard/collard or turnip greens; carrots; snow peas; jicama; or butternut squash. Use your imagination.

Mix the veggies in with the dry ingredients so the veggies get coated with the flours before you add wet ingredients.

WET INGREDIENTS

In a blender or food processor puree the following together:
- 6 eggs
- 1 large can of pumpkin (29-oz can)
- 1 cup water (or 1 cup carrot juice, but no sugary juices)

ADD wet ingredients to other ingredients and mix thoroughly. I find I have to use my hands to mix it in well as the dough is pretty stiff.

BAKE at 350 degrees until done. I use all metal mini muffin pans that bake 24 at a time and it takes 30 minutes. Use 1 level tablespoon per muffin. Before baking, make a hole in middle of each muffin with end of wooden spoon. Yield: About 110 muffins.

OATS AND FRUIT

- 4 cups old fashioned oats
- 1 teaspoon cinnamon
- ½ cup raisins
- ½ cup sliced almonds
- ½ cup dried apricots chopped
- ½ cup sunflower seeds
- ¼ cup dried cranberries

Mix all ingredients together. This will make several servings. Use as needed per these directions: Bring 1 cup water to a boil.   Add ¾ cup of the mix (or smaller proportions to fit your parrots). Turn heat to low and cook uncovered, stirring occasionally until water is absorbed, about 7 minutes. Cover, and set for about 2 minutes before serving.

CINNAMON and OATS

Cook whole oats in water with a bit of cinnamon or a cinnamon stick, coconut pieces, chopped carrots and raisins. Nice additions to the warm oats could include: slivered almonds, chopped walnuts, chopped apple or banana chunks, unhulled sesame seeds, fresh apricot or steamed pumpkin pieces.

OAT GROATS

Oat groats are sweet with a satisfying moist but chewy texture.

- 1 TBL coconut oil
- 1 cup whole oat groats
- 1 ¼ cups water or stock or juice
- ½ cup toasted sunflower seeds or chopped walnuts

Toast the groats in a saucepan stirring constantly, for about 4 minutes, or until the oats are a shade darker. Add the liquid and bring to a boil. Lower the heat, cover and simmer for about 45 minutes, or until the liquid is absorbed and the oats are tender. Remove from the heat and let stand for 10 minutes with the lid on. Fluff with a fork. Garnish with sunflower seeds or your bird's favorite condiments.

Variations: For savory oats, add some rosemary and cook minced garlic For sweet oats, add 2 teaspoons raisins, 1 cinnamon stick and 1 teaspoon orange zest.

Grains, 95

CREAM OF WHEAT DUMPLINGS
by Kathy Kocsan

- 2 eggs
- 1 TBL soy milk (or water / both optional)
- 1 TBL (or more – to taste) wheat germ
- ¼ cup Cream of Wheat
- Finely chopped parsley or basil or leafy part of celery

Stock: vegetable or chicken (any bird friendly stock to add more flavor versus plain water – which can also be used).

In a small cup/mixing bowl, crack eggs and add soy milk and/or water. Whip together with a fork until light and well blended (about a minute).

Add wheat germ and about a quarter of the Cream of Wheat, blend with a fork. Slowly add more Cream of Wheat, blend, add more, until all the Cream of Wheat is added. Let mixture rest for 5 minutes. Mixture thickens as it rests.

After 5 minutes, stir it to feel the texture. If it is too moist, add a little (just a little) more Cream of Wheat and wait a minute or two and stir again. If it is too firm, add a few drops of milk or water and stir. Should be the consistency of cake mix, maybe slightly firmer.

Heat stock in a large deep pan that has a lid (so all the dumplings have elbow room to cook and the stock won't boil over) to a low boil. With a small spoon, start spooning in the dumpling into the stock. Continue and when finished, lower heat to low and place the top on the pan. Cook for 5 minutes. Turn dumplings over and cook for another 5 minutes – no need to replace lid. Take one out and test. Should be fluffy and delicious.

My grandmother, in my eyes, was one of the best cooks in this world. She didn't need recipes, she could pinch, dash and taste and each time it would be delicious. In an effort to teach me to cook when I was young, she tried everything to help me make dumplings (which I love). I just bombed every time. One day with a smile she said to me, "we are making dumplings today with cream of wheat." You will make some that are terrible, but once you get the consistency right, it will be your dumpling. If you make it too thick, it will be hard and unpleasant. If you make it too thin, it will fall apart before it ever gets a chance to cook.

PARMESAN RICE

- ½ cup raw brown rice, cooked
- 1 egg, beaten
- ½ teaspoon celery seed
- ¼ cup Parmesan cheese, grated
- ¼ cup carrot juice

Cook the rice according to the directions. Combine the remaining ingredients and blend into the rice. Simmer very low for 5 minutes.

SESAME VEGETABLE RICE

- ⅓ cup raw brown rice. Cook according to directions.
- ¼ teaspoon turmeric
- ¼ cup unhulled sesame seeds
- Veggies such as carrots, yams, broccoli, squash. Cut to size appropriate for your parrot.

Steam the veggies until just soft. Stir the turmeric into the rice, combine with the veggies, and sprinkle with the sesame seeds.

ARROZ GUISADO (RICE STEW)

- 1 TBL coconut oil
- 1 cup brown rice
- 2-3 small tomatoes
- 2 cloves garlic
- ¼ teaspoon or less of cloves
- ½ teaspoon cinnamon
- 1 ½ cups water, or broth from cooking veggies or chicken
- ½ cup peas

Heat the oil in a large skillet over medium heat. Add the rice and saute for about 5 minutes. Combine the tomatoes, garlic, cloves and cinnamon in a food processor until smooth. Add the puree to the rice and stir, for about 3 minutes. Add the broth and bring briefly to a boil. Cover and reduce to simmer for 45-50 minutes. Stir in the peas and serve with chopped veggies and fruits, and a dollop of yogurt.

Grains,

ELIZABETH'S MASH RECIPE
by Elizabeth Bouldin-Clopton

- 1 pound white beans (northern beans)
- 1 pound green lentils
- 1 pound dried green peas
- ½ pound wild rice
- ½ pound brown rice
- 3-4 large sweet potatoes or one large can pumpkin (I often add both, although a small can of pumpkin if adding both)
- 2 bags broccoli slaw (broccoli, cabbage and carrots mixed)
- 4 grated carrots
- 2 large zucchini, shredded
- 2 large peppers (red, green or yellow, or a mix), minced (I often buy a tray of the smaller peppers in a variety of colors - some stores stock organic in the smaller peppers)
- 1 cup quinoa
- ½ cup amaranth
- ½ cup sesame seeds (hull on for more calcium)
- ½ cup sunflower seeds (if you use these for clicker training, omit)
- 1 cup slivered or sliced almonds
- 1 cup corn grits (or stone ground corn meal)
- 1 cup barley
- 1 cup steel cut oats
- 1 cup bulgur wheat
- 1 cup unsweetened chopped dates or raisins
- ¼ cup Spike No-Salt Seasoning

Rinse and pick over white beans. Soak overnight in filtered, distilled or spring water. (Tap water may contain chlorine and/or fluoride, which I do not recommend.) After 12 hours, the beans should be showing signs of plumping. Cook over low heat for 90 minutes to 2 hours, until very tender. Drain and mash lightly. (My birds eat them better mashed.)

While the beans are cooking, microwave or steam the sweet potatoes, peeling and chopping fine when cool enough to handle. Chop the broccoli slaw into small pieces. Mince the peppers. Place all in a large container. (I use two very large Tupperware bowls.) Add the nuts, sunflower seeds, dates, Spike, grated carrots, grated zucchini and sesame seeds and pumpkin, if using. If your bird is picky about veggies, you can puree them in the blender to make them smaller.

Meanwhile, in another pot, add the lentils, peas, rice, barley, oats and wheat. Cover with water plus additional water, and simmer, adding water as needed, until the lentils and barley are tender, about 45 minutes. (You need a very large pot for this.)

Cook the corn grits according to package directions, adding a little more water than the directions for polenta. Cook the quinoa according to package directions. Make sure you rinse the quinoa before cooking to prevent bitterness. Cook the amaranth according to package directions. You can cook the quinoa and amaranth together - neither takes much cooking.

Combine everything and stir! This makes a lot...plan accordingly. I then place it in quart bags, sealing with as little air as possible, lay flat to cool, and then freeze.

Every batch is different, but this is the basic recipe that I use.   The Spike seems to be especially liked - when I haven't used it they aren't as interested. You can find it in most grocery stores, just make sure it is salt-free. When ready to serve, thaw as needed, heat until warm and add fresh veggies, greens and fruit. I can always count on my crew gobbling this up. Bon appétit!

SPICY QUINOA

- 2 TBLs coconut oil (or olive oil)
- 1 teaspoon ginger
- 1 teaspoon coriander
- 1 teaspoon turmeric
- 1 teaspoon cumin
- 1 cup quinoa
- 2 cups boiling water
- ¼ cup parsley (optional)
- ¼ cup cilantro (optional)

Brown all the spices in a large saucepan. Add the quinoa and stir well. Add 2 cups boiling water, cover and simmer until the water is absorbed, about 15 minutes.

Turn off the heat and let stand for a few minutes.   Add the parsley and cilantro.   Top with other favorite condiments.

OLD FASHIONED OATMEAL

Oatmeal made from scratch is scrumptious! Use 2 parts water to 1 part rolled oats. Bring water to a boil, cook for 10 minutes. Cover and let sit for 5 minutes or so. Some birds will appreciate their own spoonful! You can add agave syrup and milk to yours.

GEORGE'S WHOLE GRAIN PILAF
by Kathleen O'Neill

George the cockatiel came to me a dedicated long-term seed eater so getting him to recognize other foods has been a challenge. He loved his pilaf though. The only difficulty with this recipe is that the grains cook for different lengths of time.

- 2 cups water
- ⅓ cup wild rice mix - I like Lundbergs which can be found at the natural foods aisle at most grocery stores
- ⅓ cup any whole grains - from the bulk grains aisle at the natural food stores - I like a mix of oat groats, wheat berries (hard wheat, winter wheat) and buckwheat groats
- ⅓ cup quinoa
- 1 carrot finely chopped
- 1-2 leaves of kale or other dark green finely chopped

Add the wild rice mix and 2 cups of water to a pot. Bring to a boil, stir once and cover. Reduce heat to simmer and cook for 20 minutes. After 20 minutes add the whole grains and chopped carrot, return to a simmer and cook 10-15 more minutes. After 10-15 minutes add the quinoa and kale and cook another 10 - 15 minute or until the water is absorbed.

MOJITO'S BULGUR, QUINOA, PARSLEY & DILL
by Carrie Baum-Lane

- ½ cup bulgur
- ½ cup quinoa
- Parsley and Dill to taste
- 2 cups of water

Boil 2 cups of water. Add bulgur, and cook for 5 minutes. Add quinoa. Cover and remove from heat. 10 minutes. Add chopped parsley and dill to mixture and refrigerate.

BROWN RICE, FRUIT and NUTS

- ½ cup raw brown rice. Cook according to directions.
- ½ cup unsulfured dried fruits, chopped to suit your parrot
- ⅓ cup chopped or crushed nuts (walnut, brazil, almond, macadamia)
- ⅓ cup unhulled sesame seeds
- ¼ cup shredded organic coconut

Combine all ingredients well. Serve with a dollop of yogurt and favorite raw or steamed veggies for a well rounded meal.   Portions can be frozen for future use.

SESAME RICE PARROT-PUFFS

- ¼ cup milk (rice, oat, almond)
- 2 eggs
- 6 TBL flour (unbleached). Good choices: ground oatmeal, garbanzo, almond
- ¼ cup unhulled sesame seeds
- ⅔ cup raw brown rice. Cook according to directions.
- ½ cup well chopped walnuts

Mix milk, eggs and flour. Combine milk mixture, sesame seeds and rice; mix well. Drop spoonful on a greased baking sheet. Bake at 350 degrees for 35 minutes. Or scoop the mixture into cast iron skillet and bake. These will look like cookies and freeze well, and they make a quick grain addition to any meal.

FLAX SESAME CRACKERS (Dehydrator)

- 1 cup flax seeds
- 1 cup sesame seeds
- 2 cloves garlic
- 1 handful parsley
- 1 teaspoon ginger
- 2 teaspoon lemon juice

Soak seeds separately for 12 hours in 2 cups water each. The flax seeds will become very gooey. Drain sesame seeds. Puree or chop garlic and parsley. Add spices and drained sesame seeds into flax goo. Mix well. Spread onto dehydrator sheet and dehydrate at 105 for 12 hours. Flip onto mesh and dry another 4 hours or until crispy.

RICE, MILLET and LENTILS

- ¾ cup dry lentils
- ¾ cup millet
- ¾ cup brown rice
- 5 cups water
- 1 teaspoon each: celery seed, turmeric, thyme
- 1 cinnamon stick
- 1" chunks of carrots (can be cut more or mashed later)

Combine lentils, millet, rice, water and spices. Bring to a boil. Reduce heat, cover and cook for 1 hour. Add carrots during last 10 minutes. Other favorite veggies can be added as well.

MILLET WITH DRIED FRUIT COMPOTE

- 2 cups water
- 1 cup millet
- 1 ½ cups dried apricots, or other unsulfured dried fruit
- 1 cup chopped nuts and seeds such as walnuts, sunflower seeds or brazil

Bring water to a boil over high heat in medium saucepan. Add millet and bring back to a boil. Chop, dice or mince dried fruit (according to your bird's preference) and add to millet. Cover, and turn heat to low. Cook about 15 minutes, or until the liquid is absorbed and the millet is tender. Stir chopped nuts into cooked millet. Top with a little vanilla yogurt.

FRUITED MILLET

- 2 cups filtered water
- ½ cup whole grain millet
- 1 large banana
- 1 cup equivalent dried, unsulfured fruit
- ¼ cup healthy nuts of choice (walnut, brazil, almond)
- ¼ cup filtered water

Combine water and millet in a saucepan. Bring to a boil and turn to simmer as soon as the cereal begins to boil. Cook covered for 15 minutes. Turn off heat and allow to rest for 10 minutes without lifting lid.

While cereal is cooking, combine banana, dried fruit, nuts and water into a food processor. Puree to desired consistency. Larger birds may prefer chunks, smaller birds may prefer a pureed mash. Feed the millet cereal with a dollop of fruit topping in the center.

TRIXIE'S FRENCH TOAST
by Laura Ford

- 1 slice sprouted grain bread
- 1 egg (for maximum nutritional benefit choose a high Omega-3 egg)
- 1 tablespoon organic juice
- Spice of choice

Beat egg with juice and add spices. Soak bread thoroughly in egg. Cook in canola, coconut or red palm oil, at medium heat, turning once, until lightly brown on both sides.

Juice suggestions: carrot juice or apple cider work best, but feel free to experiment and see what your bird likes!

Some suggested spices
- Cinnamon- antibacterial, antifungal, antiviral
- Ginger- anti inflammatory, aids in digestion
- Turmeric- anti inflammatory, antiviral
- Cayenne Pepper- anti inflammatory
- Paprika- beta carotene

QUINOA PUDDING

- 1 cup quinoa plus 2 cups water
- 1 ½ cup oat or rice milk
- 3 TBL honey
- ¼ cup almonds and/or walnuts, ground
- ¼ teaspoon cinnamon
- ¼ teaspoon lemon or orange rind
- ½ teaspoon lemon juice
- ¼ cup raisins
- ½ cup shredded coconut
- 2 eggs, beaten

Bring 2 cups of water to boil and add the quinoa; reduce heat to low and simmer for 15 minutes until quinoa is done. While quinoa is cooking combine other ingredients. Add the cooked quinoa and stir to mix. Pour into an 8 inch square baking dish. Bake for 45 minutes or until set, at 350 degrees. Top with yogurt or chopped fruit.

LEGUMES

• Kamut And Lentil Pilaf	Page 105
• Indian Lentils	Page 105
• Buddy's Cooked Beans, Grains And Rice	Page 106
• Pistachio's Rice, Corn And Beans	Page 108
• Mung Beans and Vegetables	Page 108
• Quinoa And Garbanzo Salad	Page 109
• Mung Beans And Rice	Page 109
• Oat Groats, Brown Rice And Mung Pilaf	Page 110
• Garbanzo Patties	Page 110
• Spiced Chickpeas	Page 111
• Garbanzo, Greens And Potatoes	Page 111
• Hoppin' John Salad	Page 112
• Lentil Croquettes	Page 112
• Kale and Chickpeas	Page 112
• Bulgur, Fruit And Lentil Salad	Page 113
• Pea-Laf And Brown Rice	Page 113
• Black Bean Salad	Page 114
• Garbanzo Bean Salad	Page 114
• Pureed Lentils	Page 114
• Curried Lentils	Page 115
• Coconut Lentils And Turmeric Rice	Page 115
• Greens, Garbanzo and Pomegranate	Page 115

A legume is a simple dry fruit that develops into a pod - like beans, peas, lentils, soybeans, or alfalfa. Legumes are as old as known human civilization, and often constitute a large portion of the protein requirements in the diet of many cultures.

Most legumes lack the amino acid methionine, and most grains lack the essential amino acid lysine. This is why legumes, when combined with grains, usually provide all the necessary amino acids for a perfect protein -- for example "beans and rice." The recommended proportion of legumes to grains is 1:4.

The legumes most recommended for parrots are mung, adzuki, peas, lentil and garbanzo. These can be fully sprouted or cooked. Other beans should be used only in moderation and must be fully cooked. Bean soup mixes are not the best choices for parrots, these often contain sodium and other additives.

KAMUT and LENTIL PILAF

- 15-oz can of lentils (or ¾ cup dry lentils soaked overnight)
- 1 ½ cups of kamut grains
- 2" slice of steamed sweet potato or winter squash, unpeeled and cut in chunks or pieces
- Greens (dandelion, kale, collard...)
- ½ cup unsulfured dried fruit like cherries or mango
- ½ cup walnuts
- ¼ teaspoon cumin
- ½ teaspoon or more of cinnamon

Bring 4 cups of water to a boil and cook kamut for 45 minutes until al dente. Drain well and mix in the Lentils. Stir in the sweet potato, cherries, nuts, cumin and cinnamon. Before serving, some delicious additions might be some chopped chicken, a dollop of yogurt, some fresh papaya, and/or a sprinkle of milk thistle seeds.

Can be frozen in serving portions. To warm, steam briefly, or put briefly in warm water and drain.

INDIAN LENTILS

- 1 clove garlic, minced
- 1 teaspoon ginger
- ½ teaspoon turmeric
- 1 cup cooked tomatoes
- 2 cups cooked lentils
- 1 cup frozen spinach

Combine garlic, ginger, turmeric, tomatoes and lentils. Simmer covered for 5-7 minutes. Add 1 cup frozen spinach and continue simmering for 2 more minutes. Serve with brown rice, fruit and a dollop of yogurt.

Sugar snap peas and English peas can be provided raw. Of the beans, the safest are mung, adzuki, garbanzo (chickpeas) and lentils. These can be safely sprouted or cooked. Other legumes, such as black or pinto beans, have toxic properties and must be completely cooked to be safe. Peanuts are also a legume. These are NOT recommended for parrots!

BUDDY'S COOKED BEANS, GRAINS AND RICE
by Kris Porter

STEP 1: Soak Beans

- 1 cup adzuki beans
- 1 ½ cups garbanzo beans
- About 4 to 5 whole dried red peppers

Soak beans overnight in a large pot with about 8 cups of water. Drain and discard soaking water.

Place beans in large pot covered with about 10 cups of water and add dried red peppers to season. Bring to a boil and reduce heat to a slow simmering boil. Cook for about 40 to 45 minutes. You want the beans to be done but not mushy. When finished cooking, drain and set aside in large bowl in refrigerator to cool.

Note: I find the Adzuki beans will sometimes cook faster than the Garbanzos. Often I soak them separately and cook them separately. The Adzuki beans cook for about 30 to 35 minutes and the Garbanzos cook for about 40 to 45 minutes.

STEP 2: Cook Grains and Rice

- 1 cup brown rice
- 1 ½ cups mixed grains (combination of the same grains you would use for sprouting: kamut, spelt, oat groats, triticale, wheat berries, sprouting barley
- 2 teaspoons curry powder

Place the grains and rice in large pot with about 8 cups of water adding curry powder to season. Bring the rice and grains to a boil, reduce heat and simmer until tender, about 20 - 25 minutes. You want the grains and rice to be tender but not mushy. Drain the rice and grains and set aside in the refrigerator.

STEP 3: Cook Lentils and Buckwheat Groats

- 1 cup lentils
- 1 cup raw buckwheat groats
- 1 teaspoon cinnamon

Place lentils in pot large enough to cover with about 5 cups of water adding cinnamon to season. Bring to a boil, reduce heat to a slow simmering boil and cook for about 5 minutes. Add buckwheat groats and cook for 15 more minutes. Again, cook until just tender but not mushy. Drain and add to the rice and grain mixture.

Note: Lentils cook quickly and do not need to soak before cooking.

STEP 4: Combine and Add Vegetables

In large pot or plastic dish pan, combine beans, grains and rice mixture. Add about 6 cups of finely chopped greens and vegetables. The vegetable mix can be any combination of the following: broccoli; carrots; chayote squash; turnip, mustard or collard greens; red, green or yellow bell pepper; any combination of vegetables you normally feed fresh to your parrots. If you add yams, beets or other root vegetables you should steam them first before adding to the mix. If you have some corn lovers in your flock you can add 1 cup of frozen whole kernel corn.

This is a great meal that has a combination of items from several food groups. Make a big batch and freeze portions for convenient use later.

Legumes, 107

PISTACHIO'S RICE, CORN AND BEANS
by Carrie Baum-Lane

- 1 to 1.5 cups of assorted dried beans (kidney, split peas, navy, garbanzo, pinto, lentils)
- 2 cups of rice mix. (Carrie uses a wild rice, barley mixture from Whole Foods)
- 2 chopped carrots
- 2 fresh ears of corn (cut the kernels off the cob)
- Add your bird's favorite seasonings (e.g. minced garlic, chili powder, fresh basil, sage and thyme)

Rinse beans well and soak overnight in a large pot of water.

The next day, drain and rinse twice. Leave rinsed beans in the pot and add approximately 6 cups of water.

Add chopped carrots to beans and cook for 1 hour on medium heat. After one hour, add corn, rice and seasonings. Heat thoroughly for another 10-15 minutes on low heat. Freeze portions that you can't use in a few days time. Carrie uses ice cube trays for smaller portions.

MUNG BEANS and VEGETABLES

- ½ cup mung beans
- 4 cups water
- ¼ cup diced carrot
- ⅛ cup diced parsnips
- ⅛ cup diced white daikon
- ¼ cup diced asparagus (separate stems from tops)
- ¼ teaspoon turmeric
- 1 teaspoon cumin seed
- ½ teaspoon minced fresh ginger
- 1 teaspoon ground coriander
- 1 teaspoon chopped cilantro

Combine the mung beans, water, carrot, parsnips, asparagus stems, daikon and turmeric and cook until the beans are tender. Add the ginger and cumin seed. Reduce heat to medium, add the coriander and asparagus tops, stir for 2 minutes and remove from heat. Top with cilantro.

QUINOA and GARBANZO SALAD

- 15-oz can of garbanzos (or ¾ cup dry garbanzos soaked overnight)
- 1 ½ cups of quinoa
- 2 cups mixed greens (dandelion, kale, collard, spinach or chard)
- 1 cup (unsulfured) dried cherries, chopped
- ¼ cup sliced, toasted almonds

Dressing:
- ¼ cup yogurt
- 3 TBL flax or Udos Oil
- 2 TBL fresh lemon juice
- 2 cloves garlic, minced

Bring 3 cups of water (or juice) to a boil and stir in quinoa. Reduce heat to medium low and cover. Simmer 15 minutes or until the liquid has been absorbed. Remove from heat and cool in pot.

Toss together the quinoa, almonds, greens, cherries and garbanzos in a large bowl.

Whisk together the yogurt, oil, lemon juice, and garlic. Pour over the salad, toss to coat. Dressing is optional, although the Omega oil is highly recommended!

Can be frozen in serving portions. To serve, bring to room temperature.

Before serving, some delicious additions might be some chunks of fresh fruit, sprinkle of nuts or seeds, dash of kelp or alfalfa.... Be creative!

MUNG BEANS and RICE

- ½ cup green mung beans or yellow split peas
- 1 cup water or carrot juice
- ½ teaspoon turmeric
- ¼ teaspoon cayenne

Wash the beans and discard any discolored ones. Put the beans or split peas in a pot and add the water/juice, turmeric and cayenne pepper. Bring to a boil over high heat. Reduce the heat to low and partly cover. Simmer for 30 minutes.

Separately cook some brown rice (takes 45-60 minutes).

When both are cooked, combine or serve adjacently. Beans and rice make a perfect protein. Sprinkle with other condiments like pumpkin seeds, coconut and/or chopped nuts.

OAT GROATS, BROWN RICE and MUNG PILAF

Melt 1 tablespoon of coconut oil in stove top pan. Brown 4 skinless chicken thighs sprinkled with cayenne for 5 minutes on each side. Remove the chicken from the pan.

Add 1/3 cup oat groats, 1/3 cup brown rice, and 1/3 cup dry mung beans and saute for 5 minutes or less in the coconut oil.

Add:
- 1 carrot (chopped or shredded according to your bird's preferences)
- 1 cup of sweet potatoes, winter squash and or pumpkin (cubed or shredded according to your bird's preferences)

Stir well and then add:
- ½ cup dried apricots, diced (or other unsulfured fruit)
- 1 cup juice (organic orange veggie blend or   another unfortified juice)
- ¼ teaspoon ginger
- ¼ teaspoon turmeric
- ½ teaspoon cinnamon

Bring to a boil. Add the chicken back to the pan. Cover and cook on medium low for 45 minutes. Before serving, stir in some chopped greens or broccoli chunks; perhaps a squirt of Omega oil. Top with some fresh pineapple and an unpeeled garlic clove.   Be creative! Freeze in meal size portions.

GARBANZO PATTIES

- 1 can organic garbanzo beans, well drained
- ¾ cup sesame meal or rice flour
- 2 carrots, diced or chopped
- 1 pepper (yellow or red by preference), diced or chopped

Preheat oven to 375 degrees. Mash the garbanzo beans. Blend with the remaining ingredients and shape into patties. Shape into ½-inch thick patties about 3 inches in diameter and place them on an oiled baking sheet or parchment paper. Bake for 12 minutes. Turn the patties over with a metal spatula and bake for 10 minutes longer. Remove them from the oven and allow them to rest for 5 minutes for easier removal.

SPICED CHICKPEAS
By Carolyn Swicegood
www.landofvos.com

Soak chickpeas (garbanzos) for 8-12 hours. Make sure the bowl is big enough and there is sufficient water - the garbanzos will expand a lot! Stir together two cups of drained chickpeas with a quarter cup of grated Parmesan cheese and a quarter to a half teaspoon of ground cayenne pepper (depending on how hot your parrot likes them).

- Spread coated chickpeas on a large cookie sheet.
- Bake in a preheated 350 degree oven for fifteen minutes.
- Stir well and bake for fifteen more minutes.
- Remove from oven and allow to cool.
- They become crisp and crunchy after air drying for half an hour.

These spicy, roasted chickpeas are a healthful snack for both birds and people. Try on salads as a substitute for bread croutons.

GARBANZO, GREENS and POTATOES

- 2 sweet potatoes, sliced thin
- 1 clove garlic, minced
- ¼ cup carrot, mango or orange juice
- ½ teaspoon curry powder
- ½ teaspoon turmeric
- 1 bunch mustard greens, rinse, remove stems and chop
- 1 15-oz can diced tomatoes
- 1 15-oz can garbanzo beans, drained

Bring water to a boil in a steamer with a tight fitting lid. Cut sweet potatoes in small chunks so they will steam quickly, in about 10 minutes.

While steaming potatoes, mince garlic. Heat juice, garlic, curry and turmeric in a skillet. Stir and then add mustard greens. Cook stirring occasionally until mustard greens are wilted, about 5 minutes. Add garbanzo beans and diced tomatoes. Cook for another 5 minutes. Serve greens with sweet potatoes chunks.

HOPPIN' JOHN SALAD
by Patsy Harbeson

- 2 cups cooked rice
- 2 cups black-eyed peas (dried, frozen or canned)
- ½ cup fresh lemon juice
- 2 TBL olive oil
- 1 jalapeño pepper, minced
- 1 garlic clove, minced
- ½ cup chopped celery
- ½ cup chopped parsley
- ¼ cup or more of chopped mint

If using dried peas - cook until tender; frozen peas- defrost; canned- rinse and drain. Whisk lemon juice, olive oil , jalapeño, and garlic. Stir rice, peas, celery, parsley, mint into lemon mixture. Chill at least 2 hours.

LENTIL CROQUETTES

- 1 can organic lentils, well drained
- 1 cup walnuts
- ¾ raw brown rice. Cook according to directions.
- ½ cup chopped greens (dandelion, kale, collard..)
- 2 eggs, beaten
- Shredded coconut

Mash the lentils. Stir in the cooked rice and chopped greens. Blend the walnuts into small pieces.   Stir into the lentils, rice and greens mixture.

Form into balls, dip in eggs, and roll in coconut. Bake at 400 degrees until brown, about 30 minutes.

KALE and CHICKPEAS

- 2 cups kale, cut into strips
- ½ cup cooked chickpeas (garbanzos)
- ⅛ teaspoon turmeric

Steam the kale for 10-12 minutes. Add the turmeric and chickpeas, and sauté for 2-3 minutes. Serve with a cooked whole grain like rice, groats or kamut.

BULGUR, FRUIT AND LENTIL SALAD

- 1 cup medium bulgur
- ½ cup red lentils
- ½ cup shredded carrots
- ½ cup chopped dried dates or raisins
- ½ cup chopped dried apricots
- ⅓ cup chopped parsley
- ¼ cup chopped fresh mint
- 3 TBL fresh lemon juice
- 1 ½ TBLs olive oil
- 3 TBL pine nuts, toasted

Bring 1 ½ cups water to a boil. Stir in bulgur. Remove pan from heat, cover and let stand 30 minutes. Fluff bulgur with a fork, transfer to a bowl and let cool.

Meanwhile, combine lentils in saucepan and cover with water. Heat over medium heat and cook until tender, about 5 minutes. Rinse under cold water and drain.

Add lentils, carrots, raisins/dates, apricots, parsley, mint, lemon juice, oil and pine nuts to bulgur, and toss to mix.

PEA-LAF and BROWN RICE

- 1 TBL coconut oil
- 1 clove garlic, minced
- 2 cups brown rice
- 3 cups water, or broth from cooking vegetables
- 3 TBL lemon juice
- ½ cup green split peas
- 1 teaspoon cinnamon
- 1 teaspoon cumin

In a saucepan, heat the oil and add the garlic and rice. Coat with the oil and stir for 2 minutes or so. Stir in the water or broth, lemon juice, split peas, cinnamon, and cumin. Bring to a boil briefly, then reduce heat and simmer for 45-50 minutes. Let stand for 10 minutes.

Legumes, 113

BLACK BEAN SALAD

- 1 15-oz can black beans, drained and rinsed
- 1 cup frozen organic corn, thawed
- 8 cherry tomatoes, chopped
- 1 clove garlic, minced
- ½ cup diced red bell pepper
- 2 TBLs pumpkin seeds coarsely chopped
- ¼ cup chopped fresh cilantro
- ¼ cup walnut pieces
- 1 cup chopped dandelion greens

Mix all ingredients and serve. Squeeze some lemon juice to help preserve for a couple of days. Humans can add some onions, olive oil, and salt and pepper to taste.

If freezing portions for future use, add the tomatoes and greens just before serving.

GARBANZO BEAN SALAD

- ½ cup unhulled barley. Soak for 8 hours. Rinse well.
- 1 15-oz can garbanzo beans, drained and rinsed
- 3 stalks of celery, chopped or diced
- 1 clove garlic, minced
- 1 cup chopped kale or chard
- ½ teaspoon kelp

Mix all ingredients and serve. Squeeze some lemon juice to help preserve for a couple of days.

PUREED LENTILS

- 1 small bunch Swiss chard or other greens
- 1 15-oz can lentils, drained
- 1 clove garlic
- 3 TBLs broth or carrot juice
- 1 teaspoon dried or fresh combination of thyme, sage and rosemary
- ½ cup walnuts

Puree all ingredients in a blender or food processor. Serve with brown rice for a perfect protein. Try different consistencies by adjusting the amount of broth or juice. YUM!!

CURRIED LENTILS

- 1 cup brown or green lentils (or 15-oz can)
- 4 cups + 1 TBL vegetable broth
- 1 clove garlic, minced
- 2 carrots, diced into ¼ inch pieces
- 2 celery stalks, diced into ¼ inch pieces
- 2 cups finely chopped kale
- 2 teaspoons curry powder
- 1 15-oz can diced tomatoes (do not drain)
- 3 TBLs chopped fresh cilantro

Rinse lentils in strainer. Combine with 4 cups broth. Bring to a boil and then reduce to a simmer. Cook for about 45 minutes until soft.

Heat 1 TBL broth in 2-quart saucepan. Add garlic, carrots, and celery. Sauté for a couple of minutes. Add curry powder and mix.

Add tomatoes and cooked lentils to the carrot mix. Bring to a boil, reduce heat to medium low. Simmer uncovered until lentils and vegetables are tender, about 10 minutes. Add kale and simmer for another 5 minutes. Add cilantro. Humans may want to share and season with salt and pepper, as well as sauteed onions.

COCONUT LENTILS and TURMERIC RICE

Cook together lentils, brown rice, turmeric, a couple of slices of fresh ginger, some coconut flakes, and a few cumin seeds. Lentils and brown rice usually take 50-60 minutes to cook. Make sure there is at least 5 times the amount of water to lentils and rice.

In the last 10 minutes or so, add some chopped carrot or pumpkin. When the rice is cooked, drain any excess liquid. Add some fresh cilantro and some finely chopped dark leafy greens. For a topping, add some sprouted grains, unhulled sesame seeds and a bit of flax seed oil. If you have picky eaters, top with a few seeds or nuts to motivate your birds.

GREENS, GARBANZO & POMEGRANATE SALAD

Steam 2 cups of fresh greens, like collard, kale or mustard greens. Stir in 1/2 cup COOKED garbanzo beans. Remove from heat.

Cut open a pomegranate fruit and extract the juicy seeds. Add to the greens and garbanzo bean mixture. Top with some pine nuts.

Legumes, 115

PROTEIN

- *Italian-Spiced Frittata*   *Page 117*
- *Egg Pancake*   *Page 117*
- *Birdie Frittata*   *Page 118*
- *Chicken And Peace Cereal Loaf*   *Page 118*
- *Turkey And Cranberry Loaf*   *Page 119*
- *Pumpkin Turkey Cranberry Loaf*   *Page 119*
- *Little Chicken Drummettes*   *Page 120*
- *Parmesan Drumsticks*   *Page 120*
- *Drumsticks and Brown Rice*   *Page 120*
- *Peppers And Steak*   *Page 121*
- *Chicken With Potatoes And Carrots*   *Page 121*
- *Chicken And Quinoa Salad*   *Page 121*
- *Salmon Veggie Patties*   *Page 122*
- *Seaweed Omelet*   *Page 123*
- *Frittata Muffins*   *Page 123*
- *Turkey And Pumpkin Circles*   *Page 123*
- *Chicken Stew*   *Page 124*
- *Coconut Chicken*   *Page 124*
- *Peanut Butter Coco Treats*   *Page 125*
- *Peanut Butter Corn Sticks (Treats Only!)*   *Page 125*
- *Tofu Coconut Pudding*   *Page 125*

If a bird's diet does not include pellets, and they are only eating a seed-fruit-vegetable combination, then their diet is lacking in protein. Proteins are comprised of amino acids and are the building blocks for organs, muscles, skin and feathers. Some amino acids can be created by the body, but some can only be obtained through diet.

Sources of protein include: meats, eggs, nuts, quinoa, amaranth, buckwheat, hemp seed, grain and legume combinations, and dairy products such as cheese. Dairy products should be kept to a minimum since parrots do not contain lactase, an enzyme needed for the digestion of products with lactose. Cheese, cottage cheese and yogurt do not contain lactose, but should still be used in moderation.

ITALIAN-SPICED FRITTATA
by Leigh Ann Hartsfield

*This recipe works well with a 6-inch cast iron skillet; adjust ingredients accordingly for a larger skillet.
- 3 broccoli florets
- 4-5 baby carrots
- ¼ organic red bell pepper
- 2 basil leaves
- ½ teaspoon dried oregano
- 3 eggs, or 1 egg plus ¼ cup Egg Beaters 100% pasteurized egg whites
- 1-2 teaspoon shredded Parmesan cheese
- Coconut oil
- Sprouts, for garnish

Preheat oven to 400 degrees.

Steam carrots, broccoli, and bell pepper until slightly soft. Start with carrots first, then add broccoli and bell peppers. Finely chop steamed veggies and basil leaves using a Magic Bullet or other chopper.

Generously grease skillet with coconut oil. Combine veggies, oregano, Parmesan, and eggs in a bowl. Add to greased skillet and cook on medium heat about 6 minutes or until eggs begin to firm up.

Transfer to preheated oven and bake for approximately 10 minutes, or until slightly puffed and no longer shiny. Allow to cool slightly. Slice into bite-sized pieces. Serve topped with sprouts. Refrigerate or freeze unused portion.

EGG PANCAKE

Melt a small amount of palm oil or coconut oil in a small cast iron skillet. Break an egg and stir it briefly, or add a beaten egg to the skillet.

Add chopped greens (e.g. kale or collard or dandelion).

Sprinkle condiments like cayenne, celery seed, unhulled sesame seeds.

Wait till egg is completely cooked on one side, so that you can easily flip it over and cook it briefly on the other side.

Lift out of pan, cool and cut into bite size pieces. Extra can be stored for 1 or 2 days.

BIRDIE FRITTATA
by Colleen Soehnlein

- 1 cup prepared wild rice
- 2 cups prepared kamut
- 2 TBL coconut oil
- 2 cups mixed veggies
- 8 eggs
- ⅓ cup milk

Use 2 – 8 inch round pans.
Preheat oven to 350 degrees

Prepare the kamut and wild rice. (I usually make this for the flock when I'm making wild rice mushroom soup for me.)

Break the eggs into a bowl - it's up to you if you leave in the shells. Mix in the milk – stir in the rice and veggies. Melt 1 TBL coconut oil in each pan in the oven. Pour half of the egg mixture into each pan. Bake for 15 to 20 minutes – check for firmness at 15 minutes. Cool. Remove from the pan and serve!!

CHICKEN and PEACE CEREAL LOAF

- 2 eggs, beaten
- 2 cups PEACE Cereal, crushed
  (recommend Rainforest Blend like Banana or Vanilla Nut)
- 5 TBL pure fruit juice (e.g. pineapple, mango)
- 1 teaspoon cinnamon
- 20-oz ground chicken or turkey

Preheat the oven to 350 degrees.

In a large bowl, mix together the eggs, crushed cereal, juice, and cinnamon.

Add chicken and mix gently but thoroughly. Shape into loaf on slotted baking pan or broiler pan.

Bake at 350 degrees for one hour. Remove from the oven, cover with foil, and let stand for 10 minutes before slicing to serve. Freeze portions for future use.

TURKEY and CRANBERRY LOAF

- 2 ½ pounds ground turkey meat (can substitute ground chicken)
- 2 TBLs chopped garlic
- ½ cup chopped celery
- ¼ cup chopped organic peppers (orange, red or green)
- 2 TBLs chopped parsley
- ½ cup unsulfured dried cranberries
- 1 egg
- ¾ teaspoon cayenne
- 1 cup dried fine bread crumbs

Preheat the oven to 350 degrees. Combine the chicken, garlic, celery, peppers, parsley and cranberries together in a mixing bowl.

Add the egg, cayenne, and bread crumbs. Mix thoroughly. Mold the mixture into a 5 X 10-inch loaf and place on a baking sheet. Bake for 1 hour, or until the juices run clear.

Remove from the oven and let stand for at least 10 minutes before slicing. Freeze portions for future use.

PUMPKIN TURKEY CRANBERRY LOAF

- 1 egg
- ½ cup pureed toast (whole grain bread recommended)
- 1 lb ground turkey or chicken
- 2 cups finely chopped raw pumpkin
- ½ teaspoon pumpkin pie spice
- 1 can whole organic cranberry sauce

Beat egg slightly with a fork. Stir in the bread crumbs. Mix with the remaining ingredients except the cranberry sauce. Shape into 8" round and place in shallow baking pan. Bake at 375 degrees for one hour. Spread cranberry sauce on the top of the loaf and return to oven for 10 more minutes.

Protein, 119

LITTLE CHICKEN DRUMMETTES

Submerge drumsticks in water in an adequately sized saucepan. Bring to a boil. Reduce to simmer and cook for 45 minutes. Remove skin and cool before serving. Some birds prefer to have the meat separated from the bone. Birds can be served the bones as well. Many birds will open the bone and eat the marrow. Some parrots may even eat the bone itself. Save the broth for another recipe.

PARMESAN DRUMSTICKS

- 6 to 8 chicken drumsticks, washed, skin removed
- 2 tablespoons lemon or fruit juice
- ½ cup plain dry bread crumbs or crumbs made from whole grain toast
- ¼ cup fresh shredded Parmesan cheese

Heat oven to 375°. Grease a baking dish or spray with a healthy brand of cooking spray. Roll chicken pieces in juice. Combine bread crumbs and Parmesan cheese in a shallow dish; coat chicken pieces well. Arrange chicken pieces in the baking dish and sprinkle with the remaining crumbs. Bake for 45 to 55 minutes, until browned and juices run clear when pricked with a fork.

DRUMSTICKS and BROWN RICE

- 2-½ lbs. chicken drumsticks (or drumettes)
- ⅓ cup flour (ground oatmeal or quinoa is great!)
- 3 tablespoons coconut oil
- 1 cup uncooked brown rice
- 2 cloves garlic, minced
- 2 cups sliced carrots
- 2-½ cups chicken broth, heated to boiling

Preheat oven to 350 degrees. Combine flour in shallow plate. Roll drumsticks in flour mixture to coat. Heat oil in large skillet and brown drumsticks over medium heat, turning several times, about 5-6 minutes. Meanwhile, place the rice and garlic in a 13x9" glass baking dish. Add carrots and hot chicken broth. Arrange browned chicken drumsticks on top of the rice mixture. Cover and bake at 350 degrees for 50 minutes. Uncover and bake for 15-20 minutes longer until chicken is thoroughly cooked and rice is tender.

PEPPERS AND STEAK
Gudrun Maybaum, www.totallyorganics.com

- Steak
- 1 clove garlic
- Red and yellow peppers
- Olive oil

Heat olive oil and fry garlic in it. It picks up the garlic taste, smells wonderful and gives a delicious flavor to everything you fry in this oil. Clean peppers, cut in stripes and fry until soft, though still a little crisp. I usually make this with a steak. The birds get each a few stripes of the peppers and a small piece of the meat. It is OK to add pepper before dividing the human portion from the bird portion. I add salt to my portion. It really does not need more spicing.

CHICKEN WITH POTATOES AND CARROTS
Gudrun Maybaum, www.totallyorganics.com

- ½ chicken
- 4 large carrots
- 6 potatoes
- 8 sprigs of rosemary
- 2 large cloves of garlic
- Olive oil

Heat oven to 350 degrees. Put olive oil in baking pan. Make 4 cuts into the chicken. Stuff one sprig of rosemary and ½ clove of garlic in the cuts. Cut carrots and potatoes in 1-2 inch cubes. Add to the pan with the chicken with some more olive oil and the rest of the rosemary. Depending how big the chicken is, bake 30-40 minutes. Add salt to your own portion as needed.

CHICKEN and QUINOA SALAD

- 2 cups cooked chicken, cubed, diced or shredded
- 1 cup quinoa, cooked
- 1 cup celery, chopped or diced
- ¼ cup walnuts, chopped
- ¼ cup grapes, chopped
- ¼ cup pineapple, crushed
- ½ teaspoon paprika

Combine all ingredients. Humans may prefer chilled with mayonnaise. As with all recipes, chop ingredients to the size that works best for your birds.

Protein, 121

SALMON VEGGIE PATTIES
by Kris Porter

- 1 cup cooked flaked salmon; or 1 cup canned salmon, drained
- 1 cup finely minced vegetables (collard, mustard or turnip greens; carrots; broccoli; squash; peppers; or any combination of vegetables you feed your parrots)
- 1 cup quick cooking oats
- 2 beaten eggs
- ½ teaspoon turmeric
- ¼ teaspoon cayenne pepper (or season to your taste)
- Olive oil or red palm oil for frying

DIRECTIONS

1. Remove bones from salmon and flake with a fork. If using canned salmon, remove skin and bones and drain well.
2. In mixing bowl, combine with egg, oats, and spices. If mixture is not thick enough to shape into patties, you can add more quick cooking oats.
3. Form into patties about 2 inches in diameter.
4. Fry in small amount of oil over medium low heat until brown on both sides (about 4 minutes each side)

Yield: About 10 patties. These cooked patties freeze and re-heat well. Try them yourself; they are good as they are or make a salmon patty sandwich for lunch.

NOTE: These should not be left in the cage all day or overnight. If you feed them to your parrots in their cage food bowl, change out the food bowl and cage papers after one hour. The cage papers should be changed to remove any bits of salmon that are dropped to the floor of the cage.

122, Protein

SEAWEED OMELET
Gudrun Maybaum, www.totallyorganics.com

Seaweeds are very nutritious. They contain many minerals, protein, amino acids, and vitamins like A,C,D, B complex and E. They balance the thyroid, fight free radicals, and can treat viral infections. Some are used to treat scurvy, purify the blood and much more. I mostly use purple dulse, kombu or kelp.

- 2 eggs
- 1 teaspoon of seaweed powder
- Coconut oil

Mix the eggs with the seaweed
Heat the oil in pan, pour in the eggs with the seaweed, fry one side
Turn around and fry the other side.
Cut in strips and feed to the birds, when cool.

FRITTATA MUFFINS

- 6 eggs
- 2 cups chopped veggies, such as leafy greens, shredded carrots, chopped zucchini or yellow squash.

Heat oven to 350 degrees. Beat the eggs well, stir in the vegetable combo. Oil a 12-muffin pan with canola oil. Spoon into muffin cups, about 1/4 cup each. Bake 20 minutes until set. Cool. Serve or store in refrigerator for 2 days. Freeze unused portions.

TURKEY and PUMPKIN CIRCLES

- 1 small pumpkin
- 2 cups brown rice, cooked
- 1 cup cooked ground turkey
- ½ cup fresh cranberries
- ½ cup cheddar cheese
- Paprika

Wash and cut across the entire pumpkin in 1 ½" slices. If organic, leave the peel. Remove center pulp and seeds so that the center can be stuffed. Place pumpkin rings on a baking sheet or in a shallow pan. Cook in oven for 25 minutes at 350 degrees. Mix rice, turkey and cranberries together and fill the center of the rings. Sprinkle with paprika and grated cheddar cheese. Continue baking for 15 minutes.

CHICKEN STEW
by Colleen Soehnlein

- 4 or 5 chicken legs, skinned
- Cayenne pepper
- 1 TBL coconut oil
- ½ cup lentils
- ½ cup hominy
- ½ cup garbanzo beans
- ½ cup kamut
- 1 cup blueberry or other juice
- 1 peeled and chopped butternut squash
- ½ teaspoon cinnamon & nutmeg

Soak the lentils, hominy, garbanzos, and kamut for 8 or more hours. Skin and sprinkle the legs with cayenne pepper. In a stainless steal pan – melt the coconut oil. Brown the skinned legs, about 4 or 5 minutes each side (or until they don't stick). Remove the legs from the pan. Drain the soaked beans – pour into pan and stir about for a minute. Add the chicken legs back to the mix. Add in the juice – cover and simmer for about 45 minutes. Add in the squash and cover, simmering for about 15 minutes more. Allow to cool. I usually remove the meat from the bone and mix with grains. I save the bones for the umbrella cockatoo. I do hope you'll give this a try – adjust the grains and veggies to your bird's liking.

COCONUT CHICKEN

- 2 TBLs coconut oil
- 2 pounds chicken, cut into large chunks or pieces
- 1 cup sodium free chicken broth or pure juice (mango or orange)
- 1 clove garlic, crushed or minced
- 2 TBLs freshly squeezed lime juice
- 2 TBLs fresh thyme
- 3 TBLs chopped parsley
- ½ can (13.5 ounces) coconut milk
- 1 peeled and chopped banana
- ½ cup unsalted pistachios

In a large skillet, melt the coconut oil on medium.
Cook the chicken pieces over medium heat for 15 minutes until brown.

Add the chicken broth, ½ can of coconut milk, garlic, lime juice, thyme and parsley. Mix and cover. Simmer over medium heat for 45 minutes. Stir in the bananas and pistachios. Serve with brown rice.

PEANUT BUTTER CORN STICKS (Treats Only!)

- 1 cup garbanzo bean flour or ground oatmeal
- 1 TBL baking powder
- ½ cup organic cornmeal
- ¼ cup peanut butter
- 2 TBL honey
- 1 egg, beaten
- ⅔ cup milk (almond, oat, rice, soy)

Stir the dry ingredients together in a mixing bowl. Blend the peanut butter with honey, egg and milk in a blender.   Stir the liquid into the dry ingredients.   Use corn stick or shallow muffin pans, sprayed with canola oil.   Fill each 2/3 full. Bake at 425 degrees for 12-15 minutes.

PEANUT BUTTER COCO TREATS

- ¼ cup peanut butter
- 2 TBL honey
- 2 TBL pure juice (pineapple, mango...) blended with milk powder
- 2 TBL instant milk powder
- Coconut, shredded or grated

Stir milk powder and juice together to remove any lumps. Add to peanut butter and honey In a small saucepan. Blend all of the ingredients except the coconut. Stir over low heat until the mixture is very thick. Remove from heat and stir in enough coconut to hold the mixture together so it will form into balls. Roll into a 1" balls (or whatever size your bird prefers), and roll in more coconut.   Chill several hours.

TOFU COCONUT PUDDING

- ½ pound tofu
- ¼ cup mango juice
- ½ cup shredded coconut

Blend tofu and juice in a food processor until creamy. Fold the coconut into the mixture. Top with a special treat like sprinkled cinnamon.

Index

A

Adzuki 4, 11, 24, 93, 104-105, 108
Alfalfa 9-10, 11, 17, 21, 24, 44, 104, 109
Almonds 4, 7, 11, 13, 17, 38-39, 46, 49, 50, 59-60, 62, 70-71, 73, 76, 78, 80-81, 87, 89, 91-95, 98, 101-103, 109, 125
Aloe 10, 21, 27
Amaranth 4, 11, 24, 37, 83-86, 98, 99, 116
Appetizers 17
Apple 7, 12, 38, 46-47, 55, 62, 69, 73-74, 76-79, 81, 87-88, 95, 103
Applesauce 6-7, 17, 36-38, 50, 54, 61, 70, 74-76, 79
Apricot 68, 76, 95
Apricots 4, 7-9, 11, 55, 67, 69, 72, 78, 87-88, 95, 102, 110, 113

B

Banana 7, 16, 17, 35, 38, 62, 64, 68, 70, 75, 76, 81, 93, 95, 102, 118, 124
Barley 4, 11, 23, 24, 36, 39, 41, 42, 83, 84, 85, 86, 92, 94, 98, 99, 105, 107, 114
Bread 6, 13, 26, 36, 37-38, 42, 45, 47-48, 50, 54, 56-57, 60-62, 74-75, 83, 103, 111, 119-120
Broccoli 4, 8-9, 11, 17, 25, 32, 34, 38-40, 44-45, 58, 60, 64, 90-91, 94, 97-98, 106, 110, 117, 122
Brown rice 11, 23, 36, 41, 45, 47, 55-58, 63-64, 70, 83-85, 87, 93, 94, 97-99, 101, 102, 105, 108-110, 112-115, 120, 123-124
Butternut Squash 9, 11, 34, 36, 39, 59, 64, 94, 124

C

Calcium 4, 5, 8, 17, 19-21, 24-25, 32-33, 66, 69, 77, 83-84, 86, 98
Cantaloupe 4, 9, 11, 68-69, 76, 79-80
Carrot 12-13, 26, 34-36, 39, 45, 47, 57, 61, 68, 71, 79, 84-85, 92, 94, 97, 100-101, 103, 107, 109-111, 114-115
Casserole 10-11, 34, 56
Cayenne 10, 17, 19, 52-53, 56-57, 77, 89, 91, 103, 109-111, 117, 119, 122, 124
Celery 8, 10, 12, 17, 32, 40, 46, 55, 60, 64, 80, 87-89, 92, 96-97, 102, 112, 114-115, 117, 119, 121
Celery Seed 10, 17, 20, 64, 89, 97, 102, 117
Cherry 68, 77, 84, 114
Chicken 4, 9, 11, 17, 44, 48, 51, 72-73, 88, 96-97, 108, 110, 116, 118-121, 124

Cinnamon 10, 17, 19, 37, 44, 46, 51-55, 59, 62, 66-68, 72, 74-79, 81-83, 85, 87-88, 91, 95, 97, 101-103, 105, 108, 110, 113, 118, 124-125

Coconut 6-7, 10, 17, 26, 29, 34, 37-38, 44, 46-48, 51-54, 56-57, 59-64, 67-68, 72-73, 76, 79, 81-82, 88, 92-93, 95, 97, 99, 101, 103-104, 109-110, 112-113, 115-118, 120, 123-125

Coconut Milk 34, 51, 56, 93, 99, 124

Condiments 11, 18, 35, 51, 81

Couscous 11, 34-35, 51, 56, 59, 67-68, 71-73, 83-85

Cranberries 11, 34-35, 41, 44, 51, 54, 64, 67-69, 73, 79, 87, 93, 95, 116, 119, 123

Cream of Wheat 96

Cucumber 11, 40, 49, 68, 71, 80

Cumin 45, 56-57, 63, 77, 107, 108, 113, 115

D

Dandelion 4, 8-11, 13, 27, 32, 40, 64, 91, 108-109, 112, 114, 117

Disinfect 12

E

Egg 4, 6, 9, 11, 37-38, 50, 54, 56-57, 60-61, 70, 74-5, 93-94, 96-97, 101, 103, 112, 116-119, 122-3, 125

F

Feather destructive behavior 22

Flax 5-6, 8, 17-18, 34, 38, 42, 45, 50, 57-58, 62, 64, 73, 81, 90, 109, 115

Flowers 21, 27, 30, 32-33

Foraging 7, 10, 13, 14, 15, 16, 43, 67

Frittata 116, 117, 118, 123

G

Garbanzo 4, 7, 11, 37-39, 42, 56, 61, 63, 70, 89-90, 94, 101, 104-105, 107-111, 114-115, 124-125

Garlic 10, 17, 19, 20, 27, 29, 45, 48-49, 52, 56-57, 61, 63, 72-73, 83, 87, 92, 95, 97, 107-115, 119-121, 124

Ginger 18, 44, 51, 54, 59, 61-62, 64, 71-72, 89, 101, 107-108, 110, 115

Grain 2, 4, 22, 24-25, 39, 41, 44-45, 48, 56, 61, 64, 70, 72, 81, 83-85, 88, 91-92, 94, 100-103, 106, 112, 116, 119-120

Groats 4-5, 11, 17, 23, 34, 39, 41, 44, 82-84, 86, 88, 95, 100, 104-106, 110, 112

J

Jicama 40, 80, 94

Juice 10, 13, 20-21, 26, 37-39, 41, 44-47, 49, 57, 62-63, 66-72, 74-80, 84-85, 87-88, 93-95, 97, 99, 101, 103, 109, 110-114, 118, 120, 124-125

K

Kale 8-9, 11-13, 26, 33-34, 40, 44, 49, 56-58, 64, 67, 87, 91-92, 100, 104, 108-109, 112, 114-115, 117
Kamut 4, 11, 23, 39, 44, 51, 83-86, 91, 104-105, 108, 112, 118, 124
Kelp 8, 10, 17-18, 109, 114, 123

L

Lentil 4, 11, 24, 34, 39, 76, 104

M

Mango 4, 9, 11, 26, 29, 45, 68, 69, 71-72, 76, 78, 80-81, 84, 87, 101, 108, 111, 118, 124-125
Milk Thistle 18, 60, 108
Millet 11, 17, 23-25, 82-86, 89, 94, 102
Mung Bean 4, 11, 24, 42, 76, 104, 107-110

O

Oatmeal 35, 37-38, 70, 79, 82-83, 87, 89, 100-101, 120, 125
Omega-3 8, 17-18, 45, 67, 79, 87, 91, 103, 109-110

P

Palm Oil 4, 6, 10, 26, 45, 87, 90, 103, 117, 122
Papaya 4, 9, 11, 38, 44, 79, 81, 108
Parsnips 8, 64, 66, 107
Patties 34-35, 45, 47, 57, 60-61, 89, 104, 110, 116, 122
Peanut Butter 35, 67, 76, 79, 116, 125
Pellet 9, 11, 72
Pilaf 82, 88, 90, 92-93, 100, 104, 108, 110
Pineapple 11, 38, 44-46, 54, 61, 67, 76, 78-80, 84, 93, 110, 118, 121, 125
Pinecones 10, 27
Plant 10, 23, 28-30
Polenta 68, 78, 99
Pomegranates 7, 9, 11, 68, 69, 80, 115
Probiotics 22
Pudding 82, 101, 103, 116, 125
Pumpkin 4, 5, 7-9, 11, 17-18, 20, 25, 34-35, 37-38, 44, 46-48, 51, 54-55, 61-62, 66, 68, 70, 85, 90-91, 94-95, 98, 109-110, 114-116, 119, 123
Pumpkin Seeds 5, 8, 11, 17-18, 20, 34, 47-8 51, 61-62, 85, 90-91,